TROY
REMEMBERED

by
JOHN IVIMY

Pen Press Publishers Ltd
London

TROY
REMEMBERED

JOHN IVIMY

A catalogue record of this book is available from the
British Library

ISBN 1 900796 27 9

Printed and bound in the U.K.
Published by Pen Press Ltd of London

CONTENTS

List of Illustrations
Introduction

LIST OF ILLUSTRATIONS

INTRODUCTION

Christmas Day 1990 was the hundredth anniversary of the death of a very great man. Heinrich Schliemann, the German-American archaeologist who discovered Troy and excavated Mycenae, 'made history' in the literal sense of those words. Defying the conventional wisdom of his day, he transformed what had been fiction into fact, myth into history.

Before Schliemann's discoveries the stories of the Greco-Trojan War told by Homer in his *Iliad*, and the many legends of heroes of that age that were related by poets and dramatists in the Classical Age of Greece, were held by historians to be indistinguishable from the obviously fictitious myths of the gods: there might be some elements of truth in those stories, they considered, but if so it was impossible to discover them. A veil of impenetrable night seemed to hang over the beginnings of Greek history - a veil which scholars thought would never be lifted.

Schliemann's work on the Mycenaean civilization in Asia Minor and on the Greek mainland was carried out in the 1870s. It was followed by excavations by others elsewhere in the Aegean area, and most notably by the discovery of the still older Minoan civilization by Sir Arthur Evans on the island of Crete. Evans began to excavate there in 1900. For the Cambridge historian J.B. Bury, who brought out the first edition of his classic History of Greece in that year, the Bronze Age in the Aegean was still an age of myths. Two decades later he was able to report: "The Trojan War is now recognised to be an historical event".

The giant strides thus made by archaeologists in piecing together the history of the rise and fall of those ancient civilizations have not been matched by any corresponding advance in our knowledge of the lives of the men and women who governed them. The great protagonists of the Trojan War - Agamemnon and Priam, Hector, Achilles, and the rest, are no better known to us now than they were to Aeschylus and Sophocles twenty-five centuries ago. The mists that obscure the characters of Helen (whose bid for liberation started the War) and of Odysseus (whose stratagem of the Wooden Horse ended it) are as thick now as they ever were, thanks to the fairy-tale nature of the literary sources. As Bury observed, the literary evidence embedded in myth is "harder to extract from its bed than buried walls or tombs from their coverings of earth".

It need not remain ever thus. The seven-hundred-year chasm that separated the Bronze Age civilization from the Classical was bridged by archaeology when Schliemann revealed the physical evidence. The literary or psychological evidence can, I submit, now be revealed by human memory.

So-called 'far memory', or the recollection of events experienced in a former life, is a rare faculty that can occur only in very exceptional circumstances. Some people have claimed that it can be induced under hypnosis, but such claims are doubtful and should always be regarded with suspicion. What is certain is that a great many people have experienced the feeling of '*déjà vu*' - the feeling that 'this has all happened before' - when they have encountered some situation the like of which they know they have never actually experienced in their present lives. That feeling, however, seldom goes further than that. They cannot recall the time, the place, nor any specific circumstance that would enable them to identify the former situation or event.

The ancients who believed in reincarnation attributed this blackout to Lethe, the river of forgetfulness. The human psyche, they believed, when it leaves this world passes into another realm by crossing the river Styx; and in due course - after a thousand years, according to Plato - it returns to earth by crossing the Lethe, whose waters wash away all memories of one's former lives. Lethe thus performs a useful and necessary function: that of enabling us to start each life with a clean sheet, unencumbered by memories of past errors and unhappy experiences.

This concept can be translated into modern terms by postulating that the memories of one's past experiences are housed in two 'compartments' of the brain: the grey cells of the cerebral cortex contain the thoughts and memories of one's current life, whilst the memories of former lives lie buried in the white cells that lie beneath. The two 'compartments' are separated by a kind of membrane which normally blocks the transmission of impulses from one side to the other.

Sometimes, however, a present experience may evoke by resonance a distant echo from a former life. This would account for the '*déjà vu*' sensation. Only very rarely could a clear 'far memory' burst through the membrane into present consciousness. An occasion for such an occurrence might arise when a horrendously traumatic event is experienced by an exceptionally thin-skinned sensitive mind, and a resonance is caused by the experience of a similar event in a later life.

The sack of Troy by fire and slaughter was such an event; and the mind of Odysseus, who was responsible for it, was such a mind.

It was during the bombing of London in the Second World War that I began to recall that terrible time in Troy. Once that membrane had been perforated, not only the image of the final event itself but also memories of the whole chain of events that led up to it came tumbling through, one after another in reverse temporal order, the later preceding the earlier.

In this book I have described these far memories as best I

can, using reason and imagination only where they were necessary to fill in the gaps or to explain the background. The effortless process by which the recollections entered my consciousness is described through the mouth of Odysseus in chapter 10.

This is followed in chapter 11 by a description of what I claim to be a practical experiment that was designed to prove that an individual's soul or psyche can and does survive the death of his or her body, and can return later to Earth to emerge again in the body of a new-born baby from a mother's womb. Thus, not only is reincarnation made a fact of everyday life, but the river of forgetfulness can in special circumstances be bridged in such a way as to enable a person in a later incarnation to establish his identity with his former self.

I recognise that in this scientific age no theory can be established by a single experiment, least of all a theory that denies the conventional wisdom of the day: that we only live once. To refute that belief scientifically the experiment would have to be successfully repeated at least one more time. Until that has been done the healthily skeptical reader of this book is invited to do no more than ponder the possible implications that might ensue for our modern society if the theory were to be proved and generally accepted, remembering that it has a highly respectable ancestry in the historic cultures of both East and West.

In the West the doctrine of eternal justice through reincarnation was taught by the mathematician, scientist, and religious founder Pythagoras, and by his follower, the mathematician-philosopher Plato - two of the world's most renowned thinkers.

In the East it is to be found in the oldest poem in the world, the Sumerian Epic of Gilgamesh. The poem relates how Utnapishtim (Noah) who had survived the Flood and found the secret of everlasting life, tells Gilgamesh the King, who is afraid of death, that nothing is permanent; death is like a kind of sleep.

In the most profound and spiritual of the Hindu scriptures, the Bhagavad Gita, the god Vishnu in his incarnation as Krishna, the charioteer, tells the warrior Arjuna that the Self, or Soul, is immortal; the body can be slain but not the Self, which is indestructible and eternal. Referring to his own successive incarnations he says "Many a birth have I passed through, and (many a birth) have you: I know them all, but you do not".

In the Christian religion I know of no words of Jesus which are irreconcilable with the proposition that he had reached the same conclusions as Pythagoras and Plato on this subject. The three teachers taught essentially the same morality and promised the same just rewards and punishments for individuals good and bad after their death.

That part of the Creed which requires Christians to believe in 'the resurrection of the body' is clearly absurd if it be taken to mean that bodies long dead and decayed can come to life again. For me it is credible only if it means belief in the reincarnation of the soul into the body of a new-born baby. Nor can I see how the very human founder of Christianity can truthfully fulfill his promise to return, otherwise than by being born again on a new Christmas Day.

Chapter 1
THE AGE OF KINGS

The kingdoms of the great Bronze Age civilization of the Aegean had reached the zenith of their wealth and power when Agamemnon, King of Achaea, set out from Greece in command of an allied fleet to make war on Troy. His objective was to recover Helen, Queen of Sparta, who had eloped with Paris, the debonair young son of the Trojan King Priam.

The Trojan government had rejected appeals which had been made in person by the Spartan King Menelaus in the name of international comity and public morality; and they had scorned the warning of his companion Odysseus (Latin: Ulysses) that failure to return Queen Helen would mean war, because the Greek states had bound themselves by a solemn oath to help Helen's husband to recover her by force in the event of her abduction. Priam had thus left the Greek alliance with only two alternatives: either to break their oath and submit passively to the most humiliating affront ever inflicted by eastern arrogance on western pride, or to declare war on Troy.

They chose war. The circumstances that led up to that decision, as I recall them with the aid of Greek myths, some archaeological finds and, of course, Homer, were as follows.

Helen was the youngest of a family of six high-spirited children born to Tyndareus and Leda, King and Queen of Sparta. The family consisted of two boys - the adventurous twins Castor and Pollux - and four girls, of whom the best known, both for their beauty and for their amours, were Clytemnestra and Helen.

Now, kingship at this time was only partially hereditary. It was a time when might was right, and a king's main duty was to lead his troops into battle in time of war. For this it was essential that he be a warrior of outstanding physical strength and bravery. It was the normal practice, therefore, that when a king's strength began to fail through age or infirmity he retired into private life and was succeeded by his strongest son.

In cases, however, when a king had no son who was competent to succeed, a problem of succession arose. If he had a daughter he might choose a suitable prince from another royal family to succeed him as son-in-law, but in such a case, and in cases where the monarch was childless, it was open to any athletic and ambitious prince to challenge the king's choice, or the king himself, to a trial of strength. In such a contest, which would normally take the form of a wrestling match, the kingdom was the prize for the winner, and the loser lost his life. In this way effect was given to the overriding rule of international law: the Law of Might, which declared that the strongest man had the right to rule.

Such challenges, however, were not often made, for two reasons. First, kingship was not an entirely enviable state, being both dangerous and short-lived; and secondly they were actively discouraged by the church.

The influence of religion was strongest in the early stages of the Aegean civilization's development. In those remote times all classes of the social order believed in the supernatural powers of Zeus and his family of gods and goddesses who lived on the snow-capped heights of Mount Olympus. Priests were thus able to play an effective part in promoting social harmony and international peace. The priesthood's most effective mouthpiece was the world-famous oracle of Apollo at Delphi.

As the power and wealth of the kingdoms increased *pari passu* with the expansion of their populations and their industries, so the influence of the church declined. Its decline was hastened by two great European wars that took place in the thirteenth century BC. In both, allied armies under the leadership of Argos fought to overcome the military might of Thebes. In the first, called the War of the Seven against Thebes, the allies would have been defeated but for a last minute intervention of a fresh army from Attica under Theseus, King of Athens. Soon after its arrival the Thebans surrendered, but they were not subdued. After an uneasy truce of some twenty years the second war broke out, known as the War of the Epigoni, or Successors, because its heroes were the sons of the heroes of the first war. This second war ended in a decisive victory for the allies and the sack of Thebes.

It was in the period between the wars that the mightiest of all Greek heroes, Heracles (Latin: Hercules) came to manhood. His father, Amphitryon, was a prince of the royal house of Mycenae who was living in Thebes in exile. A young man of prodigious muscular strength, it was natural that Heracles should seek another, richer, kingdom to conquer when he found there was no future for him in the now impoverished city of his father's adoption. Mindful of his ancestry, he set his sights on the kingdom of Achaea, whose capital, Mycenae, had been founded by the mythical hero Perseus and was now the greatest of all the European capitals. He set out accordingly to challenge its reigning king, Eurystheus, to a trial of strength. First, however, he went to Delphi to consult the oracle and to seek the divine blessing of Apollo on his enterprise.

In the rivalry between church and state, which then epitomised the cosmic struggle between Intelligence and Might, the church's tactics were based on deception, and the two principal weapons in her armoury were religious awe and secret

THRACE

Troy

THESSALY

AEGEAN

ASIA

Delphi

Thebes

SEA

MINOR

Ithaca

Athens

PELOP-

Mycenae

Olympia

Argos

ONNESE

Sparta

Pylos

Map of Greece and the Aegean.

information. The first was provided at Delphi by the place itself, which had been chosen by Apollo's priesthood in ancient times on account of the awesome atmosphere that pervaded its dark woods and eerie caverns under the high overshadowing cliffs of Mount Parnassus. There the Pythia, the prophetic priestess through whose mouth the god's oracular answers were enunciated, was well provided with secret information on the intimate lives of members of the Greek royal houses - information that was collected by a network of priestly spies and secretly transmitted to Delphi by carrier pigeons. [1]

When, therefore, Heracles presented himself at the gatehouse of the Delphic oracle the purpose of his visit was already known. The Pythia knew also that he was an athlete endowed with a more powerful physique than any other man in Greece, and that if he engaged the King of Achaea in a trial of strength he could not fail to win. In the games that had been held at the funeral of Pelops, King of Elis, Heracles had won every event outright. [2]

But a contest for a kingdom was not a game; and the priestess knew that the strength of Heracles' body was not matched by the strength of his mind. He was mentally unstable and given to violent fits of rage. In one of these he had hurled one of his guests down from the top of a tower, and in another he had crushed to death three of his own children. As king of a city-state he would be not only an incompetent ruler but a constant source of mortal danger to all his subjects. His reign would be a reign of terror. For the good of Greece generally and of the people of Mycenae in particular the Pythia resolved that the young man's ambition must be thwarted.

And so it was. Heracles underwent a religious experience at Delphi that changed his life.

Humbled by the awesome mystery of the place and by the oracle's solemn rituals, he listened dumbfounded to the voice of the priestess pronouncing the god's commandment. Henceforth, he learned, he must abandon the desperado's life of wild adventure that he had been living, control his anger, and apply his prodigious strength not to the subjugation of his fellow men but to the promotion of their welfare. As penance for his crimes of violence and for his arrogance in aspiring to dethrone the King of Achaea he was ordered instead to serve him as labourer for twelve years and be obedient to his every whim. If during that period he carried out faithfully all the tasks assigned him, the god promised that he would be rewarded with eternal life hereafter.

Taking the priestess's words to heart, the prince submitted himself to do the bidding of King Eurystheus, and successfully carried out one by one the famous 'twelve labours of Hercules'. And when these were completed he took up the cause of social reform.

Now, Greece at this time was the world's factory. Greek artisans had developed advanced techniques of production which resulted in Greek goods being in demand all over the known world: metal work, ceramics, textiles, leather goods, oil and oil products, and above all, ships. Great industries had been built up on this export trade, and teeming populations had come into being in manufacturing cities where workers were huddled together in conditions of the utmost squalor. Heracles' newly-developed sense of social justice was affronted by the contrast between extremes of wealth and poverty. He toured the cities and tried to persuade the ruling class to ameliorate the conditions of their workers. When he failed in this, he addressed himself direct to the workers and incited them to demand better conditions. He invented a practical way in which they could insist on their demands being met. Pointing out that the rulers were wholly dependent on the willingness of the workers to continue working, he organised the mass withdrawal of labour from one industry after another, keeping the men idle until he had wrung from their employers the concessions he demanded. "Your oppressors," he would say to the men, "will submit to nothing but force. That is the only language they understand. They have armed themselves with spears and swords; I am now arming you with a blunt but heavier weapon. In refusal to work you have a massive club with which you can give them a clout on the head they will never forget." Thus was invented the industrial strike, which came to be known as "Heracles' club". It was a weapon which the hero used fearlessly and with powerful effect in every part of Greece, incurring the hatred of kings and princes but worshipped as a god by millions of poor people. The founder of the first socialist movement, he acquired a numerous following of people who called themselves 'Heraclids', or 'children of Heracles'.

These Heraclids tried to establish their subversive doctrine in Mycenae and other cities of the Peloponnese, but they proved such a thorn in the side of the ruling class that king after king expelled them from his territory, and they were driven to take refuge among the Dorians of Thessaly in the north. There they founded a socialist republic and gathered strength for a further assault on the southern monarchies.

The Greeks of the Classical Age, who had no conception of the problems of an industrial society, thought that Heracles' famous 'club' was a real club, and that the Heraclids were the real children of Heracles, whence that hero was credited with the performance of feats of sexual virtuosity no less prodigious than those of his reputed father Zeus. (It was said that Zeus became enamoured of Heracles' mother Alcmena and deceived her by disguising himself as her husband Amphitryon while the latter was away. Such was the god's ardour that he turned day into night and spent the whole of thirty-six hours in love-making in order to procreate so mighty a hero.)

The most lasting contribution that was made to Greek civilization by Heracles was his invention of the Olympic games. Although he himself, the greatest athlete of all time, had forsworn the right to challenge a king for his throne by a trial of muscular strength, he was concerned to ensure that when others exercised that right the contests were fairly held and fairly judged. He recalled how one king - Oenomaus, King of Elis, who had no male heir - had held on to his kingdom well past his prime by requiring any challengers who sought to inherit it by marrying his daughter Hippodameia to compete with him in a chariot race across the Peloponnese. The king gave his challenger a good start. But he was a furious driver, and since his horses were the finest in Greece and his chariot was lighter because his contestant was required to carry the not inconsiderable weight of Hippodameia in the chariot beside him, he invariably caught up on the first uphill gradient. But he did not overtake, for as soon as he came within striking distance he hurled his spear and transfixed the young man through the heart from behind. The heads of a dozen or more hopeful athletes whom Oenomaus had dealt with in this way adorned the gates of his palace.

But eventually Oenomaus met his match. The Asian prince Pelops (who gave his name to the Peloponnese) bribed the royal chariot-master to remove the metal linchpin from one of the king's chariot-wheels and substitute one of wax, which melted when the axle got hot. In the resulting crash Oenomaus lost his life. Pelops married Hippodameia and became by international law the rightful heir to the Kingdom of Elis.

To the earnest mind of Heracles this kind of contest was not cricket. He decided that the system of king selection must be the next target for his reforming zeal. Choosing a moment when the throne of a certain kingdom was about to become vacant, he organised an athletic contest on the Elean plain, to which competitors were invited from all over Greece. His idea was that the winner should have his name put, as it were, on a waiting list for the vacancy, being honoured meanwhile with a laurel wreath as his prize. The name of Heracles as judge and organiser of the games would be a guarantee that the winner was in fact the best athlete in all Greece and therefore the fittest man to be king.

These first games were successful, and Heracles erected a shrine to Olympian Zeus on the site where they were held. To this day the place is known as Olympia. Despite their success, however, no further games were held there for a long time. The international situation was drastically changed by the outbreak of the second war against Thebes.

Out of that war a new and baleful star arose and blazed with burning heat in the firmament of power politics: Diomede, son of Tydeus, a man of unbridled ambition, cruel, ferocious, and vindictive. His family came from the wild west. His father Tydeus had been heir to the Kingdom of Calydon in Aetolia but was banished for murder. He found refuge in Argos and took part as one of the Seven in the first Theban war, where he fought with unprecedented savagery. When mortally wounded by a blow from Theban Melanippus, Tydeus found the strength to fight back and kill his slayer, from whose severed head he proceeded as he died to tear out the brains with his teeth.

After his father's death, Diomede had been brought up as an orphan in exile, despised and ridiculed for his Aetolian accent and rude manners by the lordly aristocracy of cultured Argos. They called him 'the Calydonian boar', after the animal for which his country was famous. When the second war broke out he joined in and fought with the same ferocity as his father had done before him. No man could stand against the weight of his massive bronze-tipped spear as he hurled it with prodigious force. His onslaught was like a hurricane; the enemy's ranks scattered, and strong men fled in terror at the sound of his coming.

When, shortly after the destruction of Thebes, the throne of Argos fell vacant, Diomede claimed it, and no one dared to challenge him. But his ambition did not stop there; rather did his success whet his appetite for more. The Kingdom of Argos at that time covered only the southern part of the province of Argolis, the north being part of the more powerful kingdom of Achaea. The two capital cities, Argos and Mycenae, were only six miles apart. Diomede looked with greed and envy on the towers of the famous hill city of Perseus which dominated the Argive plain.

The news of his accession sent a wave of fear through Mycenae, now ruled by the pious, high-minded King Agamemnon, son of Atreus and grandson of Pelops and Hippodameia. Agamemnon took immediate steps to increase the size of his army and to negotiate a ring of alliances with neighbouring states who felt themselves threatened by the dreaded son of Tydeus. Arcadia in the centre of the Peloponnese was a traditional ally of Argos, but the western and southern states of Elis, Pylos, and Sparta were now, with Achaea, welded by Agamemnon's diplomacy into a united front of unassailable strength. The key state in this alliance was Sparta, both because of its size and strength and because it had a common boundary with Argos. If Diomede attacked Mycenae he would expose himself to an attack by Tyndareus, King of Sparta, in his rear. To cement the Achaeo-Spartan alliance, Agamemnon married Tyndareus' beautiful elder daughter, Clytemnestra. A brilliant wedding was arranged in Sparta to which all the crowned heads of Europe were invited. It was the most glittering social event of the century.

A balance of power was thus established, and an uneasy peace was maintained. Both sides built up their forces. Agamemnon worked hard to maintain the alliance, while Diomede brooded like a tiger at bay how to escape from the iron ring that had closed round him.

A sudden stroke of fate played into the Argive chieftain's hands, upsetting Agamemnon's carefully laid plans and precipitating overnight the greatest international crisis that Europe had yet known. The twin sons of Tyndareus, Castor and Pollux, were killed in a brawl, and the aging King of Sparta was left without an heir. Diomede saw his chance. Invoking the ancient Law of Might he claimed the right to succeed to the throne of Sparta and to marry the King's only unmarried daughter, Helen. Everyone knew that if the claim were refused, Diomede would assert it by force. If it were granted, the crowns of Argos and Sparta would be united and constitute with Arcadia a combination powerful enough to overwhelm Mycenae. In that case, Agamemnon could not afford to wait for Diomede to consolidate his new power; he would make a pre-emptive strike at once. Either way, therefore, a third great war seemed inevitable.

In an atmosphere of mounting tension, all eyes were turned on Princess Helen.

SOUTHERN GREECE showing possible State boundaries in 1200 BC.

Notes on Chapter 1 - The Age of Kings

1. It is not to be expected that any direct evidence will be found in Greek literature to support this description of the 'secret service' of the Church of Apollo, because the probable fate of any person suspected of betraying a religious secret in those days was for his dead body to be found by the wayside with one of Apollo's arrows through his heart. The inferential evidence is as follows:

   a. Pigeons or doves were sacred to Apollo.

   b. Hawks, which might prey on doves, were likewise sacred, which explains why falconry was never practised in Greece although it was a popular sport in Persia and in Egypt, and it was introduced in China about 2000 BC.

   c. The presence of large numbers of doves in the precincts of the Delphic oracle was such a notable feature of the site that the prophetic preistesses were themselves often popularly referred to as 'the doves' (Greek: peleiai)

   d. The fame of the oracle could never have spread so far or lasted through so many centuries if there had not been a strong element of magic that convinced even hardened skeptics that the priestesses were indeed divinely inspired.

   e. The procedure for consulting the oracle required the suppliant to spend some time at a distant gate-house, where he was questioned before setting out alone for the shrine. The inference is that this procedure was designed to enable information to be passed from the gate-house to the Pythia by telecommunication before the suppliant reached the shrine, so that she could not only prepare a good answer to his question but also astound him by revealing an intimate knowledge of his thoughts and aspirations such that it seemed impossible it could have come from any purely human source.

f. This theory could explain why no literature was produced in Bronze Age Greece. Being the source of their power and wealth, knowledge of the arts of reading and writing was kept a closely guarded secret monopoly of the priesthood.

2. Velleius Paterculus I. viii.

Chapter 2
THE MARRIAGE OF HELEN

The name of Helen, daughter of Tyndareus and Leda, was known far over the civilized world not only for her beauty but even more for her vivacity and wit.

When she was nine years old, Helen fell in love with the most popular idol of the times - Theseus, King of Athens - and ran away to marry him. She got safely to the Attic frontier, but at the first town she came to inside Attica the mayor detained her while he sent word to Tyndareus, who despatched her twin brothers Castor and Pollux with all haste to fetch her home. Back in Sparta she told a lurid tale of how the Athenian king had sent men to abduct her by force and was going to keep her in prison until she matured; and although Theseus had in fact never even set eyes on her, his reputation with women being what it was, Helen's story stuck. It was brought up eight centuries later and used as propaganda by the Spartans when they were at war with the Athenians.

But the episode that spread her fame across the world was the affair of the egg.

It was Helen's first dance in Sparta's royal palace. Every year Tyndareus and Leda gave a party for the palace staff at which it was the custom for the younger members of the royal family to dance with the servants. Helen in a décolleté dress looked radiant. She lost no time in singling out the best-looking of the young men present and gave him every encouragement to become familiar with her. He was a young groom employed in her father's racing stables. During an interval she took him out onto the verandah and asked how he liked her dress. He took his cue and went on to admire her hair-do. She obviously liked compliments. Emboldened by her response he came a little closer and looked into her eyes. He had had a little wine, the night air was warm and fragrant, and the sound of music could be heard through the open portico.

"I think you're divine," he said, "how did you get those lovely eyes, and that lovely neck? It's so long and white... it's ...it's like a swan's."

He was astonished at his own boldness and delighted with his simile; he had never said anything so poetic before. But Helen decided he was going too far. When he came close a strong whiff of the stables reached her nostrils. She did not mind him admiring her neck but she objected to his breathing down it. She decided to make a fool of him.

"Yes," she said, "of course. Didn't you know?"

"Know what?"

"About my father."

"What about him?"

"Well, you see, it's like this. You won't tell anyone, will you? My real father is Father Zeus. When the King was away one night Zeus fell in love with my mother and flew down to her in the shape of a swan, and... well... that's why my neck is so long and white."

He looked at her incredulously.

"I know it's hard to believe," she went on, "but you see, my mother really was very pretty before she got so fat. Zeus, you know, is terribly fond of pretty women."

"You don't mean Zeus is really your father? I don't believe it."

"Yes I do. Honestly."

"But how could you possibly be sure? I mean, the King could still really be your father, couldn't he? You can't prove he isn't, can you?"

Helen thought fast. "Well, as a matter of fact I can," she said triumphantly. "You see, what happened was this. *Exactly* nine months after the swan came Mummy laid an egg, and that was me."

The young man was dumb-founded. The girl looked straight into his eyes, a perfect picture of wide-eyed innocence.

"I promise you it's true," she said, keeping her fingers crossed behind her back.

"I just can't believe it."

"All right, don't if you don't want to. But don't blame *me* if Father Zeus punishes you for not believing in his powers."

As she spoke she listened, half hoping that Zeus would punish *her* by showing his anger in a clap of thunder. Then she would have felt that her lie had been atoned for and everything would be all right. But the sky was serene and no sound came except the sound of music and laughter from the great hall. The last thing she said was "You'll promise you won't tell anyone, won't you?"

"Of course," he said, "I promise."

And of course he broke his promise.

A few days later a little girl came shyly up to Helen as she was walking in the street with her sister Clytemnestra.

"Please, your Highness," she said, "could I ask you a favour?"

"What is it?" enquired Helen.

"Please could you let me have a piece of the shell?"

"Shell, what shell?"

"Please, miss, the shell of the egg what you was bor...er... hatched out of. You see, Mummy says it's impossible and even if the Almighty begging his pardon did come like a bird the Queen couldn't lay an egg but Daddy says everything's possible with the gods and if you said it was true then it must be 'cos you're a princess and you ought to know but Mummy still won't believe it and they're quarrelling something dreadful they are, so just to prove it Daddy says could you let him have a piece of the shell so he can show it to her." She paused for breath. "I promise he'll give it back," she added.

Leda and the Swan. Roman limestone relief. Crete.

Helen was nearly crying with laughter but managed to control herself.

"I'm terribly sorry," she said, "but we haven't got it now. You see, my mother didn't want the King to know about Zeus' visit so the shell had to be thrown away at once. If the King ever got to hear about it he would be very angry."

"I should think he would indeed," said Clytemnestra when the girl had gone away and Helen had explained what it was all about. "What's more, I hope he does find out and spanks you jolly hard. You've got the whole town laughing at him by now."

Before long not only the aristocracy of Sparta but sophisticated high society all over the world was holding its sides with laughter; for Clytemnestra told the boys, and the boys told their friends, thinking it the funniest thing that had ever happened. They ragged their good-natured mother mercilessly. For her next birthday they gave her a dinner service with a pattern of swans, designed to their order. The idea caught on, and soon swan pattern china was the rage in all the palaces of Greece. No one with social ambitions could afford to be without it for their drinking parties.

Amongst serious-minded people lower down the social scale the story of Leda and the swan became a matter of violent controversy. Few of them doubted that a god could assume the shape of a bird if he wanted to, and have intercourse with a woman; the question in dispute was: if he did so and the woman conceived, would she have a baby in the normal way, or would she lay an egg? Those who believed that with gods all things were possible were in the egg school of thought; but others did not believe that gods had it in their power to interfere to quite that extent with the course of nature. The dispute went on for a long time and caused many a heated argument. It was the first great public controversy between Science, which is commonsense, and Religion.

King Tyndareus himself, a kind-hearted but eccentric and irascible monarch, never heard how he had been made to look foolish, because no-one ever told him. All he knew was that in Helen he had a daughter who was renowned for her wit and beauty, and in Castor and Pollux he had two sons who were no less well known for their practical jokes and daring escapades. Their fearlessness and sense of fun endeared them to the country people and in due course won for them a place in the sky as the Heavenly Twins. But once they went too far. As guests at the joint wedding of their two cousins they ran off with the two brides in the middle of the festivities. The joke was not appreciated. The irate bridegrooms gave chase; and in the ensuing fracas, Castor and Pollux lost their lives.

Diomede, King of Argos, lost no time in issuing a challenge to Tyndareus to face him in a trial of strength for the throne of Sparta, or else to cede the throne to him without a fight by giving him the hand of Helen in marriage. Tyndareus rejected both alternatives. It seemed to him inevitable that eventually he would have to submit to Diomede's ultimatum, but he could at least buy time; and there was always a chance that some other young prince might come forward who could outmatch the Argive king in strength of muscle. Following the precedent set by Heracles he announced that on a certain date an athletic contest would be held in Sparta, the winner of which would receive Helen as his bride with the Kingdom of Sparta as her dowry.

Kings and princes from every corner of the Greek world accepted the challenge. Never before had such a brilliant galaxy of noble manhood assembled together to compete for so dazzling a prize. There was great Ajax, son of Telamon, King of Salamis, and his brother Teucer the archer; Menestheus who had succeeded Theseus as King of Athens; Patroclus son of Menoetius, King of Opus; the lesser Ajax, King of the Locrians;

Antilochus, son of great Nestor of Pylos; lordly Idomeneus, Crown Prince of the ancient Kingdom of Crete; and twenty or thirty other famous heroes. They came in the shining strength of manly youth, bearing rich gifts each according to the wealth of his kingdom; but excelling all alike in strength of sinew and in the magnificence of his gift, was the sinister figure of Diomede, King of Argos.

Tyndareus' son-in-law, Agamemnon, came from Mycenae to watch the contest, and with him was Nestor, the aging King of Pylos, the most experienced warrior in Greece. Another distinguished spectator was Tyndareus' brother, Icarius, whose self-effacing and rather plain daughter Penelope was a constant source of comfort and support to her cousin Helen at this time of anxiety and fear.

The four men spent many an anxious hour discussing the merits and prospects of the numerous contestants as they watched them at practice in the fields. Often hopes would be raised as one or another accomplished some new feat of strength or speed. But always the ferocious Diomede strode forward to eclipse the record by a still mightier feat. There seemed to be no way out. If the contest was fairly judged, Diomede was certain to win. And Agamemnon left no one in doubt that if Sparta were joined to Argos, he would declare war at once. He strongly urged the claims of his brother Menelaus as a sensible, courageous, honest young man who would rule well and ensure the continuance of the Achaeo-Spartan alliance. Tyndareus replied that he would be very willing to hand over his daughter and his kingdom to Menelaus, but he dare not. The young man was no athlete. He was a small man who talked in a loud voice but packed little power behind his punch. His chief interest and skill lay in horses and chariots which occupied his time to the exclusion of other forms of exercise. If Tyndareus gave Menelaus the prize without his

Two examples of swan pattern drinking vessels of Mycenaean design
found in the remains of Philistine cities in Canaan. c.1200 BC.
Similar examples dating from the same period have been found at other
places round the Eastern Mediterranean.

having won it in open competition Diomede would have no difficulty in wresting it from him.

Agamemnon, a deeply religious man, then suggested that they should consult the Delphic oracle. Icarius and Nestor agreed. But Tyndareus only snorted. He loathed "those damned sorcerers with their mumbo-jumbo" as he called priests, and he never allowed any of them to come near his palace.

The four men sat on in gloomy silence. It was a hot sultry afternoon in August, two days before the contest was due to take place. From a seat in the shade of an oak tree they were watching Diomede and Menelaus practising spear-throwing. Diomede had just thrown, out-distancing the other's modest throw, but Menelaus in a loud voice accused him of cheating by having both feet over the line when he threw. The two men were shouting at each other and it seemed as if they would come to blows. The four men on the bench looked at each other in disconsolate silence. They did not notice one of the other contestants detach himself from the field and walk slowly away in the direction of the house, carrying his tunic on his arm, his head bowed in thought.

Odysseus, son of Laertes, was a person of no importance. His father was King of Ithaca, a small rocky island off the north-west coast. It was a poor kingdom which few people from the mainland had heard of and hardly any had visited. Nor was the young prince distinguished as an athlete. He could run fast in a sprint, and sometimes by a cunning trick he could fell a stronger man in wrestling, but he was no good at throwing or boxing. A shy young man with a mathematical mind, he had accurately assessed his chances of winning the contest as nil and had not even brought a present. He had come simply because everyone else had come and because his father had sent him, not wishing his son to be left out of the most momentous royal event of the age. Like the rest, he fell in love with Helen as soon as he saw her face and heard her voice; but he subdued his emotions, and when he saw the princess in company with her gentle cousin Penelope it was the shy figure of the latter that attracted his gaze.

On this sultry afternoon, as a line of turret clouds rose like a battlement on the western horizon portending thunder, Odysseus sensed the tension in the air. His nerves were on edge and his head ached. When the two men started quarrelling he decided to go in; he could not stand discord. On reaching the palace he entered the great hall, leaving his tunic, his only garment, on a chair by the door. The athletes practised in the field naked and the young man should have put his tunic on before approaching the house; but he was very hot and he knew there would be no one about at that hour; the old men were out watching and the women were upstairs resting. He poured himself a cup of water from the ewer on the hall table, and sat down to drink. Presently Leda's little dog came up and put a bone down at his feet, wanting to play. Odysseus picked it up and sent it sliding over the polished marble floor, it came to rest against the far wall underneath an oak chest where the dog could not reach it. The young man had to lie flat on his face with his arm outstretched in order to recover it.

In this ungainly position, with the dog yapping at his elbow, Odysseus did not hear the rustle of silk on the stairs behind him. He got up to find Queen Leda standing at the foot of the stairs, between him and the entrance. To get to his tunic he had to pass close to her. There was no other cover, and any attempt to hide his nakedness would, he thought, only serve to draw attention to it. He decided to stay where he was and to act normally as if he were fully clothed.

Leda tried to ease his embarrassment.

"Feeling unwell?" she asked.

"Yes ma'am. I had a headache and came in for a drink of

water," he answered. Their eyes met. She gave him a kindly smile, and his heart went out to her.

"I'm sorry," she said. "I came down because I saw you coming across the lawn and I wanted to talk to you. I heard shouting out there in the field and I was afraid. Are they fighting already?"

"No only quarrelling, as usual."

"Oh dear, I'm so afraid. Odysseus...," her voice was anxious and appealing, "they say you're clever. Can't you think of some way out? There must be a way out. Surely there hasn't got to be war. Everything will go. All this..." indicating the great hall which to her was the embodiment of civilization. "The King and I are sick with worry. We can't think any more. But you... you're young... perhaps you can think of something. Do please try... please".

He was moved by her appeal.

"I know how you must be feeling," he said; "we all feel it too. Perhaps there may be a way... I don't know. I'll think."

"Yes please, do think."

She turned away as he moved forward to pass her, making for the door. Half-way up the stairs she turned back and watched him as he picked up his tunic, slung it over his shoulder, and went out. A shaft of sunlight glistened on his small well-shaped buttocks. On a sudden impulse she called him back.

"Odysseus."

He turned round. "Yes ma'am?" he answered.

She hesitated, changed her mind, and was silent. For a brief moment Leda had forgotten she was a queen and knew only that she was a woman. But his deferential "ma'am" reminded her of her position.

"Was there something else?" he asked.

"Oh...no...nothing. Just do try and think of some way out, please. That's all."

"I'll do my best," he said, wondering vaguely what it was she had been going to say.

From her window Leda watched the young man walk pensively across the lawn. She sighed.

"What a pity," she thought, "what a pity he's so nice. Or is it?"

That night a heavy thunderstorm broke over the palace. As Odysseus lay in bed listening to it he thought over the events of the day. He was conscious of having broken a strict social convention, but Leda had not reproved him. She had pretended not to see. He owed her a debt which he felt obliged to repay.

He thought about her problem - the problem of peace. A war between Argos and Mycenae would be no light affair. It would be a long and terrible struggle in which nation after nation would be dragged in. For months past every valley in Greece had been ringing day and night with the hammering of iron on bronze as swords and spears were being forged in preparation for the slaughter. Who could say where it would end, or what kind of civilization would be left when the dead had been counted?

It was obvious that no solution could be found within the framework of existing international politics. There had to be a new approach. Odysseus remembered having once seen a brave man running for his life pursued by a swarm of angry hornets. Diomede may be stronger than anyone else, he thought to himself, but he is not stronger than all the rest of us together. If before the contest all the competitors were to swear an oath to combine with one another to attack anyone who tried to take Helen or her kingdom away from the man to whom she was lawfully given in marriage, not even the son of Tydeus would dare to challenge such a combination. It would be a league of kings sworn to band together against aggression. A new principle would be established for the preservation of peace: the principle of collective security.

Early next morning Odysseus requested an audience with the Queen. He found her sunk in a state of despair, but at the sight of him she brightened. He explained to her briefly his idea, and she took him at once to King Tyndareus. It took some time for the King to grasp it, but at length he was impressed. For the first time a ray of hope gleamed in the darkness. But there was a major difficulty.

"This idea of a league of kings is all very well," said Tyndareus, "but I can't stop the games now, and I've got to give the prize to whoever wins. The problem is how to prevent Diomede from winning."

"I have a plan for that too," said Odysseus.

"Oh have you?" said the other eagerly. "Let's hear it."

The young prince explained his plan. "There are to be ten contests altogether, are there not? And you want Menelaus to win, don't you? Right. I propose that you don't rank all the contests equally but allot a number of points to each and award the prize to whoever wins the most points. I suggest you allot five points for each of the first nine contests, and fifty for the chariot race, which comes last. Menelaus is a fine charioteer, and if you make sure that he has the fittest horses and draws the most favourable starting position he ought to win. It won't matter then if Diomede wins all the other nine contests; Menelaus will still get the prize."

Tyndareus looked at him blankly.

"You see," Odysseus went on, seeing the older man's difficulty, "nine fives are only forty-five."

"Oh," said Tyndareus, "I think I'm beginning to see."

Odysseus' plan was approved. On the morning of the contest a solemn ceremony was held at which one of Tyndareus' race-horses was sacrificed. The King himself swore to give his daughter Helen in marriage to the winner of the games and each contestant swore to protect her against any man who sought to take her away from the successful suitor.

The result of the games was much as expected. Diomede won eight events; the weight-lifting contest was won by great Ajax, and the chariot-race by Menelaus. There was little air of expectancy amongst the athletes as they assembled in the great hall in the evening to hear Tyndareus name the winner. That Diomede's name would be pronounced seemed a foregone conclusion. When, therefore, Tyndareus, with Nestor and Agamemnon standing close behind him, called out the points and proclaimed Menelaus the winner it was as if an electric shock passed through the assembly. Rigid and tense, every man looked at Diomede. There followed a moment's silence which seemed an eternity. Then Diomede spoke in icy tones.

"You are mistaken, noble Tyndareus. There were ten contests of which I won eight. I claim the prize by right of conquest."

"Not so, noble Diomede," replied the King of Sparta. "I have counted the points and yours is the second prize. Is that not so?" He turned to Agamemnon and Nestor who echoed assent. "A handsome prize it is too; a hundred fat oxen, a mighty shield of triple leather and bronze chased with silver, of the finest workmanship, and a woman skilled in all kinds of handicraft. The first prize, as I have said, is awarded to Menelaus, son of Atreus, who has fifty points against your forty.

"This is a cheat," replied the other. "If you persist in this trickery, I shall challenge Menelaus to face me in mortal combat."

"Then remember the oath," said Tyndareus. "Every man here is sworn to come to the aid of Menelaus if anyone seeks to take away his prize."

"We swore to defend the rightful winner of the games,"

replied Diomede through clenched teeth. "Menelaus is not the rightful winner. Do you dispute that I won eight events?"

The King did not answer, and Diomede went on: "Then I am the winner and the prize is mine by right. It is me, not Menelaus, they are sworn to defend."

Tyndareus was nonplussed. After a whispered consultation with Agamemnon who, like him, was unable to think of an answer, he called in desperation to Odysseus who was skulking at the back of the crowd.

"What say you to that, son of Laertes?"

Odysseus suddenly found himself the centre of attention, with all eyes focussed on him. He hated the limelight at the best of times, but now, with the whole world hanging on his lips he could have wished that the earth would open and swallow him up. His mouth was dry and his heart was pounding. But he kept his head.

"The words of the oath," he began in a thin voice that sounded far away. He stopped and cleared his throat. "The words of the oath," he repeated more clearly, "were to defend him who is rightfully *declared* the winner. I think there can be no doubt that the right to declare the winner belongs to your Majesty as King of Sparta and master of the games, and since your Majesty has declared Menelaus the winner, it is him we are sworn to defend."

Diomede turned on the speaker in a burst of uncontrolled rage.

"Dog," he shouted, "you lie. The oath was to defend the rightful winner."

During the long silence that followed, the peace of the world was balanced on a knife-edge. Every man stood stock still, listening only to the pounding of his own heart. Somewhere in the distance a horse neighed. At last the massive figure of great Ajax, son of Telamon, towering above the rest, moved forward.

"Odysseus is right," he said slowly. "It is for our host the noble Tyndareus to decide who has won the right to receive the hand of his daughter, the fair Helen, in marriage. He has declared Menelaus the winner; and it is not meet for any one of us to question his decision. We are now sworn by our oath to come to the aid of Menelaus against any man who seeks to take the prize away from him. I for my part will abide by my oath."

Idomeneus said he agreed with Ajax, and there was a general murmur of assent.

The trap had closed. Diomede was like a hungry tiger whose prey has been snatched out of his jaws by a force that he knows is stronger than himself. Hatred and rage blazed in his eyes and choked his voice.

"This is not the end," he threatened. Then, fixing his steel grey eyes on Odysseus, "You will pay for this," he hissed, and stormed out of the hall.

Tyndareus realised too late the danger to which he had exposed his guest. As a measure of protection he invited Odysseus to stay on after the others had gone. Leda acknowledged gratefully the debt that not she only but the whole of Greece owed to his resourcefulness. International peace was preserved and the tension relaxed. For the first time collective action has been successfully organised to prevent a war - the 'War of the Spartan Succession' that never was - and to deter a would-be aggressor. But though the wild beast had been caged, he had not been tamed. Removed from the political arena, the struggle was now focussed into a personal feud between two men. It was a struggle between Intelligence and Might, the eternal earth-centred struggle of the Universe.

In recognition of his service, Odysseus was asked by his hosts if there was anything he wanted in return. Yes, there was. He asked for, and was granted, the hand of Penelope in marriage. The wedding was arranged quickly and quietly while preparations were being made for the marriage of Helen and Menelaus. Helen acted as Penelope's bridesmaid. Those who watched her during the ceremony noticed that her eyes were moist, her smile was forced, and once or twice she wiped away a tear.

When the bridal pair departed, Tyndareus sent a military escort to accompany them to the port of embarcation. He gave Odysseus, as he thought, a kindly piece of parting advice.

"If I were in your shoes, my boy," he said, "I would take care to avoid finding myself alone with that fellow Diomede on a dark night."

Odysseus smiled wanly. It was September; and a cool breeze was blowing from the east, the first presage of the coming winter. With a slight shudder, he pulled his cloak closely about him and drove off westward with his bride.

Chapter 3
THE ELOPEMENT

The thirteenth century BC in Greece was a period of rapid technological development which led to an explosive increase in population. The discovery of ways of smelting iron and the invention of iron tools - the metal was as yet too precious to be used for any other purposes - caused a revolution in manufacturing processes comparable to that which has been brought about in modern times by machine tools. On the basis of this new and so far exclusively Greek technology a thriving overseas trade developed in which Greek manufactured products were exchanged for food and raw materials. By the end of the century the population of Greece was far in excess of what the country could support from its own resources, and the Greeks were dependent on foreign trade not merely for their luxuries but for the very necessities of life.

As merchant ships in those days seldom ventured far out of sight of land, Greek traders looked for their markets along the northern shores of the Mediterranean. They developed two great trade routes, named after the principal cargoes which were carried on them, the Amber Route and the Gold Route. The first ran westward round the shores of the Adriatic to Istria, at the mouth of the Po, and far down the coast of Italy where a vigorous new civilization was already in the adolescent stage. The second and more important trade route ran east through the Dardanelles and into the Black Sea, connecting with ports on the western shores up to the mouth of the Danube and along the southern shore as far as Colchis at the foot of the Caucasus.

By 1200 BC hundreds of Greek ships were passing through the Dardanelles every week bringing to the Argive port of

Nauplia gold, silver, iron ore, timber, hemp, corn, and many other essential commodities, and returning laden with oil and all manner of manufactured goods. But trade difficulties were already beginning to be experienced. While the demand for imported materials continued to rise with the expansion of the Greek population, the market for exports declined, partly because of rising costs at home which resulted from frequent strikes, and partly because the eastern peoples were themselves learning western manufacturing techniques.

During the time that the European trading empires were being built these eastern peoples were weak and divided. The Sumero-Babylonian empire had fallen and the empires of Assyria and Persia had not yet arisen. The interior of eastern Anatolia was under the dominion of the Hittites, a strong military power which was in alliance with Egypt, but the western end of the peninsular, with the Aegean littoral, was divided into numerous separate kingdoms which had acquired a veneer of western culture from frequent contacts with their Greek neighbours. The ruling families of these states were strongly westernized. They spoke the Greek language fluently, adopted Greek customs and manners, intermarried freely with the Greeks and often sent their sons to be educated in Argos or Mycenae. From trade contacts these Asian rulers learnt Greek law and business methods, whilst many of the ordinary people had been converted to the worship of Greek gods.

One such westernized state was the Kingdom of Ilium, or Troy, on the river Scamander in the extreme north-west corner of the Anatolian peninsular. Troy was a wealthy city whose ruler derived a fabulous income from the sale of a liquid which gushed out of the ground without any effort on his part. The ruler was King Priam, and the liquid was water, which he sold to Greek ships passing through the Dardanelles. As Troy, on the river Scamander, commanded the only source of fresh water for a long sailing distance in either direction, Priam was able to charge a scarcity price for his asset. From the enormous revenues thus effortlessly acquired he built a magnificent palace within a fortified citadel, and for the large population which collected round it he employed western architects and town-planners to lay out a fine city of broad streets and modern buildings outside the fortifications.

To meet the increasing costs of maintaining this affluent society Priam periodically raised the price of water, until a point was reached when the Greeks decided to build bigger ships which were capable of negotiating the passage of the Dardanelles without having to stop for water at the Scamander. Finding themselves thus faced with the loss of their main source of revenue, the Trojan government, whose foreign policy was now controlled by Hector, the strongest of Priam's fifty sons, negotiated a union with the King of the Thracian Chersonese (the Gallipoli peninsular) on the other side of the strait, and then announced that the Dardanelles was a national waterway belonging to the Thraco-Trojan Union and that no foreign ships would be allowed to pass through it without payment of dues.

The Greeks were at once angry and alarmed. Hector, they said, had placed his thumb on Europe's windpipe. They denied his right in international law to interfere with the freedom of shipping in the straits and they demanded that he rescind his decree. When he refused, Diomede of Argos attempted to seize the straits by force, but his move was condemned by Agamemnon. Less directly concerned than Diomede because Achaean trade was mostly with the west, the high-minded King of Mycenae preached the peaceful settlement of international disputes, deprecated the use of force as repugnant to enlightened opinion in that modern age, and expressed the hope that some other solution could be found. These sentiments had their effect on public opinion in Argos. There were many heated exchanges between the Greek rulers but no agreement was reached, and Diomede's attempt aborted.

Hector had scored a diplomatic victory over the West. His decree, being backed by force, became legally binding, and Greek merchantmen had no option but to pay the dues. Observing his success, other eastern rulers put up their prices against the Greeks and banded together to defend themselves against possible reprisals. Anti-western sentiments, instigated by Hector, spread through Asia and even infected the continent of Africa. Peoples who for generations had been accustomed to accept the fact of European superiority became suddenly aware that the West was not invincible. They were reminded of many insults they had suffered in the past from European arrogance, and were encouraged by the example of Troy to assert their independence of the men they had so long regarded as their masters. The successful nationalization of the Dardanelles sent a shudder of unrest through the civilized world, portending a mighty shift in the balance of power as the estern giant, refreshed after centuries of sleep, rose to his feet and prepared to measure his strength against the western giant who, having exhausted his spirit in centuries of progressive effort, was now sinking into decline.

Many people on both sides were oblivious to the gathering storm. Business in the great cities of the three continents was more prosperous than ever before. Money flowed freely. There was laughter and merriment and carefree abandon as men and women ate and drank, danced, sang, and made love. Even the poor prospered.

The smart set in Troy was led by Paris, a younger son of King Priam. Gay and debonair, artistic, imaginative and romantic, he was the exact opposite of his humourless and politically ambitious half-brother Hector. With plenty of money and nothing to do he dabbled in many different pursuits. At one time he took up drawing and painting. Then he fell in love with a shepherdess, Oenone, and lived with her in a pastoral idyll, composing poetry while they tended sheep on Trojan Mount Ida. Tiring of the squalors of country life, Paris abandoned Oenone and returned to the city where he took up singing and acting. Then one day he decided to go on a tour of European capitals, and came presently to Sparta where he was received in fitting style by King Menelaus. He had heard numberless tales of the beauty and wit of Queen Helen - who had not? - and the desire to meet her was not the least of the motives which led him to Europe. But he little thought that within a few hours of their first meeting he would have lost his heart to her, and she hers to him.

When Helen and Paris met it was as if a long-hidden key had been found to a door that opened onto the garden of love. It was a garden full of laughter, for each found in the other a perfect foil and stimulus for their scintillating sense of fun. How dull now seemed Oenone's lyrics, how boring Menelaus' endless talk of chariots and horses! By way of excuse to prolong his stay in Sparta Paris obtained her husband's permission to paint Helen's portrait. As luck would have it, Menelaus had to visit Crete for the funeral of his grandfather before the portrait was finished. Blinded to his wife's attachment by his own conceit, the tactless man invited Paris to stay on and finish the portrait while he was away.

Within twenty-four hours of the King's departure, Paris and Helen were on their way to Troy. News of the elopement spread through Greece like fire through a parched forest. Helen was not only the Queen of Sparta; she was the pride of all Europe.

The whiteness of her skin and the quickness of her wit had become symbols of the supremacy of the European race. Her abduction by a dark-skinned Trojan princeling was therefore felt by citizens of every Greek state as a personal insult to themselves. There was talk of immediate war, but opinion was divided. In every city there was a war party and a peace party. Menelaus was for war and called on his brother Agamemnon to back him. This time the King of Mycenae, his personal honour at stake, was prepared to take action. He proposed sending an ultimatum to Priam giving him ten days in which to return Helen or face war. But Mycenae could not move without Argos, and Diomede did not conceal his pleasure on hearing that the prize he had so eagerly sought for himself had been snatched away from the man who had cheated him of victory. He was also glad to revenge himself on Agamemnon for opposing him when the vital interests of Argos were at stake in the Dardanelles. So he refused to go to war for Helen.

The two sons of Atreus now decided the time had come to enforce the treaty by which Helen's suitors had bound themselves before the contest for her hand. If all the others agreed to honour their oath, Argos could not afford to stand out alone. First they obtained the support of old Nestor of Pylos. Then they visited Odysseus, to whom Laertes had now handed over the kingdom of Ithaca. Odysseus was known throughout Europe as the architect of peace and was therefore the man to whom peace parties in all countries would be likely to turn for leadership. If Odysseus admitted to being bound by the treaty in the present circumstances, unforeseen though they were at the time the oath was taken, the peace parties would be deprived of their strongest argument, and the war parties would gain a leader whose resourcefulness would be of inestimable value in organising the expedition.

Now Odysseus had no doubt that he was bound by his oath to go to war for Helen if Menelaus called on him to do so. But he was no soldier, and he had no army to speak of. He hated the very thought of fighting and feared he would show himself a coward in battle. Above all, he dreaded the prospect of coming face to face with Diomede. So when he heard that Menelaus and Agamemnon were coming to try to enlist him he decided to say No. Ithaca had no quarrel with Troy.

When the two brothers arrived, they found Odysseus in a field wearing a peasant's cap, ploughing with an ox and an ass yoked together and flinging salt over his shoulder as he went. He suspected they wanted him for his brain, so he was pretending that his brain had gone. But when Menelaus put Odysseus' baby son Telemachus in front of the team, he snatched it up and so proved himself sane. [1]

The sons of Atreus were insistent that the terms of the treaty that Odysseus had himself devised to establish the principle of collective security must be strictly observed. Priam would laugh in the face of a divided Europe, but if the western powers showed themselves united in a strong resolve to see justice done he would not dare to refuse their very modest demand for Helen's return.

It was finally agreed between the three men that, provided the other principal Greek kings agreed, Menelaus and Odysseus would visit Troy on a mission to bring Helen home, with power to warn the Trojans that if they refused to let her go the Greeks would come in force to take her. In undertaking this mission Odysseus realised that it would involve him in making a speech to an assembly of the Trojan people - a prospect that alarmed him only slightly less than that of fighting a battle. Silently he made a pact with his favourite deity, Athene, the warrior goddess of wisdom, that if she helped him to get through his speech successfully he would, if called on, go to war in reliance on her ability to see him safely through that greater ordeal as well.

Helen and Paris, sailing east under a cloudless sky, had no conception of the commotion that their elopement was causing behind them. A gentle westerly breeze just filled the sail and wafted them smoothly from island to island across the blue Aegean. Paris was content to sit with his arm round his beloved, watching the seagulls wheeling peacefully overhead. If he thought at all of the political effects of his voyage, it was to congratulate himself on a fine achievement. Eastern queens and princesses had on several occasions in the past been carried off by Greek adventurers; his abduction of Helen was a magnificent piece of tit for tat. He anticipated with a thrill of pride the admiration he would receive when he returned home with the Queen of Sparta, Europe's most famous beauty.

But Helen was uneasy. She had acted on an impulse, without thinking, and now that she had time to think she was unhappy. What would people say at home? What would they think of her in Troy? What would her husband do? She now regretted her hasty decision but was too proud to admit it. She tried to justify her conduct.

She sat silent for a long time, unusually thoughtful.

"What's the matter?" asked Paris. "You're so serious today."

"I've been thinking," she said. "What will your father say when he finds out who I am? Do you think he'll be angry and send me straight home?"

"Not a bit of it. He adores having beautiful women around him."

"But he won't want to offend the Greeks, and after all I am a reigning Queen. There's public opinion to think of, too. I wish I could think of some plausible excuse for running away."

"Don't worry, darling. Just let the people see you and know that we love each other and they'll never let you go back to that old bore of a husband of yours."

"Now I've got you I don't really feel he's my husband. It's not as if I had chosen him myself, is it? I was awarded to him as a prize in a competition, that's all. It's time men were made to learn that some women have minds of their own and object to being treated like cattle. I might have been given to anybody."

"Exactly. You had no choice at all. Your fate rested on the knees of the gods."

Helen laughed. This was a new expression she had not heard before. In her irreverent mind she pictured a lot of naked gods sitting in a row with a scroll marked "Helen's fate" resting on their nobbly knees.

There was a pause. Suddenly she looked up and asked:

"Do you believe in gods?"

"Well no, not really. Why?"

"Good," she said. "That makes it easier."

"Make what easier?"

"I'm just thinking. Gods are supposed to be stronger than men, aren't they?"

"Why, of course. But what on earth are you driving at?"

"Supposing the gods had awarded me to you as a prize in a competition, you would then have a stronger right to me than Menelaus has, wouldn't you?"

"But why should I be competing with the gods about anything? Gods don't compete with men."

"You might have been judging a competition between them, mightn't you? Didn't you say you used to write poetry to them on Mount Ida?"

"Well, yes, I did. But that isn't much of a qualification." He paused. "Now if you'd said goddesses, that's a subject I can honestly claim to know something about. As an expert on the female form I'm regularly in demand at home for judging the annual beauty competition."

"Oh, you are, are you?" snapped Helen. "I'm not sure I shall let you go on with that. We'll see. Anyway, goddesses will do splendidly for our purpose. Suppose Hera, Athene and Aphrodite came and asked you to judge which of them was the most beautiful..."

"I'd choose Aphrodite every time."

"That's just what I thought. And she could promise you..."

"...the most beautiful woman in the world as a reward." He hugged her. "Darling, this is terrific. Do let's go on."

By the end of the voyage they had worked out all the details of the story that was to become known as the Judgement of Paris: how Discord, piqued at being the only immortal not invited to the marriage of Peleus and Thetis, threw a golden apple amongst the wedding guests, marked "For the most beautiful"; how the three goddesses disputed which should have it, and how Hermes took them to Paris when he was tending sheep on Mount Ida and asked him to judge, Hera promising him power if he would give her the apple, and Athene wisdom. If he were asked why he had said nothing about this at the time, Paris would say that when he gave the apple to Aphrodite she had made him swear to secrecy until she had fulfilled her promise by delivering to him the most beautiful woman in the world. He could never have brought back Helen if he had announced his intention of doing so beforehand.

When the couple reached Troy everything went as planned. No rumour of the elopement had preceded them. When Helen accompanied Paris into Priam's palace she drew admiring looks from all sides, but in accordance with the custom of the times no questions were asked until after they had had a bath and a meal. Then after dinner, King Priam and Queen Hecuba, Hector and his young wife Andromache, other princes, princesses and elders of the people sat round in the great hall to hear Paris tell his story. A good actor, he told it with a straight face. But once when he was describing the judgement scene Helen could suppress her laughter no longer; she exploded in a loud guffaw which would have given the show away if she had not succeeded in disguising it as a smothered sneeze.

When the recital was over there was a barrage of questions.

"What did the goddesses wear?"

"I asked Hermes to invite them to undress. That was essential if I was to judge them properly, and they agreed."

"How close did they come?"

"Aphrodite came very close indeed."

"Did you touch her?"

"Of course not. That would have been most improper."

And so on.

Old Priam, that fiery, cunning, laughter-loving sheik, was not taken in, but he was delighted by his son's audacity and was astute enough to know that public opinion on both sides would demand some explanation of his conduct. He laughed loud and long and congratulated Paris on his excellent taste in women. But Hector was angry. "I don't believe a word of it," he said. "The Queen of Sparta must go back to her country at once." He was scared of a major international crisis, but no one else took his view. The elders took their cue from Priam who they could see had been completely captivated by Helen's charm. In the end the King gave his decision.

"The Queen of Sparta is an honoured guest in our country," he said. "She is welcome to stay in our humble palace for as long as she cares to grace it with her lovely presence."

Helen thanked him gracefully. "I am sure I am going to be happy here," she said. "But please don't call me the Queen of Sparta any more. I have left my country for good. In future my home is here in Ilium."

"What shall we call you, then?" asked the King.

"From now on," she answered, "I wish to be known as plain 'Helen of Troy'.

Note on Chapter 3 - The Elopement

1. This story comes from Hyginus, a Latin author who wrote a book
   of collected Greek and Latin myths in the first or second century
   AD. I have no recollection of the incident myself, but I have no
   doubt that Odysseus did somehow try to feign insanity in order
   to avoid the obligation to join the forces that Agamemnon and
   Menelaus were collecting.

Chapter 4
THE WARNING

A few weeks later a more serious debate took place in the Trojan council chamber. Menelaus and Odysseus had arrived on their mission and were invited to address the council.

Menelaus began. He talked boldly and in loud tones on an emotional level about honour and love and duty and chivalry. He used some forthright language about Paris's abuse of Spartan hospitality, and he appealed to the Trojans, who set high store by their code of hospitable conduct, to redeem their honour by punishing the criminal in their midst and restoring Queen Helen to her lawful husband. What, he asked, would be the Trojan reaction if he, Menelaus, were to abscond with the fair Andromache?

It was a moving speech and the cabinet was deeply impressed. If the matter had been left there, they would have let Helen go. But it was now the turn of Odysseus to speak.

Odysseus spoke nervously, gripping his staff tightly in his hand and keeping his eyes fixed on the ground for fear that if he looked at his audience he would lose the thread of what he was saying. It was Priam's cousin Antenor who afterwards described the effect of his speech on the assembly. "The words of Odysseus," he said, "were like snow-flakes in winter." [1] They were soft and gentle and ice-cold, and they struck a chill in the marrow of those who heard them.

Odysseus made no appeal to the emotions. He avoided making moral judgments. He was not concerned with questions of right and wrong but kept strictly to facts. He described the state of feeling not only in Sparta but all over Greece and explained the terms of the treaty by which Helen's suitors had bound themselves. He reminded his hearers of the sense of frustration previously felt in Greece over the nationalisation of the Dardanelles, and he described the new preparations for war. He warned them plainly as a statement of simple fact, that if Helen were not returned there would be war. It would be war on a scale never before imagined. No man could tell where it would end or who would win, but of one thing he was certain: war would bring tragedy to the lives of countless men and women. It might even be the end of western civilization, to which Trojans and Greeks alike belonged. But if Helen returned to Sparta with her husband, he foresaw a long period of peace and friendship between the nations. It was for Troy to decide.

Odysseus had prepared his speech carefully. He faltered for words only once and quickly recovered himself. When it was over he said a silent prayer of thanks to Athene for helping him. He and Menelaus went straight from the council chamber to the market-place and there addressed a gathering of the common people, telling them exactly what they had told their rulers and bidding them pass the news on.

Meanwhile in the council chamber the Trojan leaders debated anxiously. Hector was angered by Odysseus' speech. His pride was hurt. "Trojans do not give way to threats," he told the council. But Priam and the others were in favour of a peaceful settlement if they could return Helen without loss of face. Helen herself had now made this possible by asking to be allowed to return to her husband. She said she had had a dream in which Hera and Athene had appeared to her; they were angry at Paris's judgment and told her that a calamity would fall upon Troy if she remained there. She was genuinely penitent for all the trouble she had caused and wanted to put it right.

But when it was discovered that Odysseus had been talking in public and all Troy knew that war was being prepared there was a sharp revulsion of feeling. The Trojans could not now return Helen without losing face. They would seem to be yielding to a threat of force and their self-esteem would be irreparably damaged. Troy's national prestige was at stake. Hector sounded his allies and ascertained that the eastern states were ready to back him solidly if the Greeks attacked. Puffing out his chest, he made a patriotic speech saying the Trojans were a proud people; they were not to be brow-beaten by threats. If a Greek force dared to set foot on Trojan soil they would be sent reeling home with a bloody nose.

Hector's speech was loudly cheered by the majority. But a thoughtful minority were doubtful of his wisdom. They viewed the future with dark foreboding. Wise Antenor in particular urged Priam to swallow his pride and let Helen go. But Priam would not listen.

The King sent for the Greek envoys and told them that their ultimatum, as he called it, was rejected.

Menelaus and Odysseus argued no more. The speeches were over. The time had come for action.

Troy had been warned.

Note on Chapter 4 - The Warning

1. *Iliad* 3. 216-224.

Chapter 5

WAR

The expeditionary force which the Greeks sent to Troy to recapture Helen was too small for its purpose, disunited, unorganized, and incompetently led. It was not so much an army as an assemblage of national armies each under the independent sovereign command of its own king. The only organisation which held the forces together was a council of kings presided over by Agamemnon who was recognized as the leader of the expedition and given the title "Anax Andron". This might be translated as "Commander-in-Chief of the Allied Forces", although Agamemnon had no power to command any contingent except his own Achaean army, nor would he have dared to give orders to such doughty warriors as Diomede of Argos or Idomeneus of Crete on how they should dispose their troops.

Agamemnon had no talent for planning military operations, but in the course of ten years of war he acquired considerable skill in the art of humouring refractory monarchs. His greatest asset was his strong force of character, founded on integrity and sincerity of purpose springing from deep religious convictions. A simple man, perplexed by complicated situations that he could not wholly grasp, he leaned heavily on the advice of others. But though simple he was not without conceit. As Commander-in-Chief of the biggest armed force that had ever yet been assembled, he took a lofty view of his responsibilities, refusing to concern himself with matters of detail and confining his attention to questions of general policy affecting the war as a whole. Thus he never saw those little cracks in the enemy's defences which a good general could have used to secure a leverage whence to crumble the whole edifice. Seeing only the overall picture, somewhat blurred in outline, he could think only in terms of frontal assaults on the main force of the enemy, a method which tended to consolidate rather than disrupt the latter's resistance.

Agamemnon's principal adviser on operational matters was old Nestor of Pylos, a man of unrivalled military experience and gifted with a retentive memory which enabled him in any crisis to recall, and recount at length, how he had dealt successfully with an analogous situation in some former war. Unfortunately he was never able to appreciate that the conditions of this war were different from those of previous wars, nor did Agamemnon realise that all Nestor's memories of past operations would have been well sacrificed for one sensible plan for a future operation.

To advise him about the will of the gods Agamemnon had on his staff the priest of Apollo in Mycenae, Calchas, who saw in this appointment an opportunity for him to restore some of the influence that used to be exercised by the church over the rulers of Greek states but which was now practically dead.

Calchas had been partly instrumental in starting the war, for when Agamemnon was still debating with the other leaders whether or not to declare war on Priam, he had been sent to Delphi and had returned with the prophecy that Troy would fall. But the baleful effect of his influence was not fully felt until the expedition was about to set sail from the beaches where it assembled at Aulis in the Euboean strait. Adverse winds prevented the force from sailing, and when several days went by with no change in the weather, Calchas was asked the reason. He answered that the goddess Artemis was angry, and would be placated only if Agamemnon sacrificed to her his most precious possession: his daughter

Iphigeneia. Torn between faith and doubt, between love and duty, and influenced by fear of his atheist wife Clytemnestra, Agamemnon at first refused, but later was prevailed on to obey when he found he was being accused throughout the army of being responsible for the delay. Iphigeneia, consenting, was led to the altar. The priest cut her throat and poured her blood on the ground as a libation to the goddess. At the back of the crowd that watched the ceremony, Odysseus turned his eyes away and swore eternal enmity to organized religion.

The Greeks made a successful landing against opposition on the beaches at the mouth of the Scamander. In the battle for the beachhead a new figure came to the fore, proving himself the mightiest warrior that had yet appeared, a more formidable fighter even than mighty Diomede. Achilles, son of Peleus and Thetis, was the leader of the Myrmidons from Thessaly. Too young to have been one of Helen's suitors, he was now, at twenty, the finest athlete of all the Greek leaders, excelling them both in the strength of his chest and arms and, even more, in the swiftness of his feet. He was the fastest runner yet seen on earth and he used his speed brilliantly in unorthodox tactical manoeuvres in battle. But in spite of his unrivalled capacity as a warrior his presence at Troy proved of little use to the Greek armies. For Achilles had been spoilt in his early childhood by his indulgent father and a timid tutor, Phoenix, to whose care he had been entrusted after his mother died; and now he was moody, obstinate and uncooperative. He had a fierce temper which he had never learnt to control. Accustomed always to having his own way and to be given everything he asked for, he was incapable of working as a member of a team. Indeed, he regarded it as necessary on principle that he should disagree with every one else. For when his mother, Thetis, was drowned in a bathing accident from which her body was never recovered, his father had shirked telling him the truth and had led him to believe that she had not died but was immortal, being a daughter of Nereus, the old man of the sea, and had swum away under the water to live in her father's house for ever. As half an immortal, Achilles considered it would be improper for him ever to admit that he could be wrong about anything or not know in every situation what was best. In any discussion he would take a different view from everyone else and when he did not get his way he would storm out of the room like an offended prima donna and sulk.

Achilles was the hero of the battle for the beachhead. But the victory was not followed up. The Greeks pitched camp in the plain of Troy not far from their ships on the left bank of the Scamander, which then flowed in a channel some way east of its present course just under the walls of the city. No attempt was made to organise any services for the camp as a whole. Each contingent was responsible for its own supplies and services. They even chose their own camp sites independently of one another. When quarrels arose, as they often did over administrative difficulties, the rule was that the smaller contingent gave way to the larger. On occasions when it was imperative that an independent decision should be taken to secure fair play for one of the smaller contingents the only man who ever came forward to propose a sensible solution was Odysseus. Odysseus thus became, in effect, the self-appointed Officer in charge of Administration for the Allied Forces in Asia.

Winter turned into summer and summer back to winter and the war dragged on year after year, a recurring tale of muddle, quarrelling, and useless sacrifice. Achilles went off for a year or two on a war of his own, ravaging the coast lands south of Troy. Although his departure deprived the army of its most potent striking force, the other leaders were not sorry to see him go. They sent for huge reinforcements from home. The Trojans called for more help from their allies. Year by year the armies grew, until by the tenth year the Greeks had over a hundred thousand men in the field, and nearly twelve hundred ships were drawn up on the beach in two ranks two miles long. But there was no strategy, no master plan of attack; just fruitless struggles to kill the enemy and gain a little ground.

Meanwhile at home economic difficulties were mounting. The drain of manpower and resources produced many shortages, and prices rose sharply. There were frequent strikes. The authorities took stern measures and sent all Heraclids, or strike-leaders, into exile. But many people were starving and there was no money left to pay for imports of food.

Anxious consultations took place amongst the Greek leaders. Capital levies were ordered by the principal allies, and private hordes of gold were confiscated. Towns and villages in Asia far away from Troy were ransacked for food and clothing and anything else they possessed that could help to relieve the distress of the demoralised armies.

In the tenth year of the war inadequate food, bad sanitation and over-crowding at length produced the epidemic that Odysseus had long feared. Agamemnon did not know what to do. The inference was that Apollo was angry. Calchas was consulted, but the only effect of the advice he gave was to produce a quarrel between Agamemnon and Achilles which resulted in the latter sulking in his tent and refusing to fight.

Hector now took advantage of the Greek weakness to launch a mighty counter-offensive. In one day the Trojans drove the Greeks from the city right back to the sea, a distance of some five kilometers, and would have broken through the rampart which protected the Greek ships had not darkness intervened. That night there was consternation in the Greek camp. Agamemnon and Nestor called a council of war. Unable to think of a plan of their own, they proposed to try to find out what were the plans of the enemy by espionage inside the Trojan camp.

When Agamemnon called for volunteers to go on this dangerous mission the only man who responded was the intrepid Diomede. But Agamemnon would not let him go alone. He invited him to choose one of the other leaders to accompany him. Diomede was silent for a while. Then a sudden thought struck him. Looking round the company his eye fell on the man he sought, and in the commanding tone of a judge delivering sentence of death on a convicted criminal he called out: "I choose Odysseus."

During the ten long years of the war, Odysseus had studiously avoided the company of the Argive King. He knew that Diomede had neither forgotten nor forgiven; that he had been waiting, waiting and watching, for the hour of his revenge. Now, with a sick feeling in the pit of his stomach, Odysseus knew that that hour had come. Bitterly he recalled the parting words of Tyndareus, who had brought this on him, "If I were you I would take care to avoid finding myself alone with that fellow Diomede on a dark night." Now here he was, condemned to be alone with Diomede on a dark night, *and on a battlefield*.

The stage was set for murder.

Chapter 6
THE SCAPEGOAT

Once again all eyes were focussed on Odysseus to see how he would answer. Everyone knew that Diomede had made his choice for one reason only - revenge. This time the Ithacan would find no safety in numbers. He had been challenged to a duel - a fight to the death in single combat; and no one doubted that, if Odysseus accepted the challenge, as it seemed he must, his wiles would avail him nothing. As the weaker man he must succumb.

Desperately Odysseus tried to think of some way of escape. He thought of pleading illness, but he knew that they would know that was a lie. That was the way of cowardice; and he dared not confess himself a coward before this assembly of warrior kings. He could think of no other excuse. The council waited tensely in silence for his reply.

At length, in a hollow voice Odysseus gave his answer: "Very well, let's go."

Armed only with their naked swords, the two men set off into the night. For a while they ran side by side, picking their way among the corpses that lay strewn on the battlefield. When they reached the path by the city wall they turned and ran along it in single file, Diomede dropping behind and leaving Odysseus to set the pace. In mounting fear Odysseus ran as fast as he could, increasing the distance between them. Diomede stumbled. Recovering himself, the strong man increased his speed and closed in on his quarry.

Now he was within the distance of a sword stroke, and Odysseus sensed the arm already raised to strike the fatal blow. Controlling his terror in a supreme effort of will he turned to face the murderer.

As he turned, his eye was caught by a dark figure approaching from the opposite direction. Running with his head down, the man almost collided with him. As he passed, Odysseus called "Halt there!" and caught him by the arm, but the man broke free and ran off into the darkness. The two Greeks gave chase and Diomede caught him. They questioned him. His name was Dolon, son of Eumedes, a wealthy noble. He had been sent by Hector to spy on the Greek camp, being promised the horses of Achilles as his reward for finding out how the Greek ships were guarded. Now, shivering with terror, he fell on his knees and begged his captors to spare his life.

But Dolon's fear served only to draw down upon him the fury of the frustrated murderer. With one sweep of his sword Diomede severed the man's head from his body. It fell in the dust while the tongue was still giving utterance. [1]

As Dolon's soul sped from his body in death, Odysseus felt his heart lightened, as if a burden had been lifted from him. His fear left him, and he knew that he was safe. Diomede was standing facing him, the blood dripping from his sword. The passion had left him and he was uncertain what to do.

The two men stood facing one another, and though they could scarcely see in the darkness, their eyes met and something passed between them. Diomede knew that Odysseus knew he had meant to murder him, and he dropped his gaze. It was Odysseus who broke the silence.

"Come on," he said, "let's get going. It's your turn to run in front this time. I'll follow." And when the other hesitated, "It's all right," he continued, "have no fear. I'm not going to kill you."

The strong man did as he was told.

The voice that spoke those words of command Odysseus did not recognise as his own. It was as if some other man within him, a man he did not know, had taken occupation of his body. That man did not then depart but remained with him, and Diomede looked on this new Odysseus in awe as a man who was indeed protected by some god. Thenceforward the two men became friends, and when, during the battle for the ships that followed during the next few days, Diomede was wounded, it was Odysseus who risked his life to cover his retreat, and himself suffered a wound in so doing.[2]

In the same battle Agamemnon, too, was wounded. With the Greek Commander-in-Chief and his two mightiest warriors, Achilles and Diomede, out of the fray, the Trojans redoubled their efforts, and this time they succeeded in penetrating the rampart and were within an ace of setting fire to the Greek ships. In this extremity, when the Greeks were on the point of utter defeat, it was Odysseus who saved the day. He knew that battles are lost and won in the minds of the opposing commanders before the decisive blow is struck, and he took his place beside the Commander-in-Chief. When Agamemnon all but panicked at the sight of Hector charging forward irresistibly with a firebrand held aloft, and was about to give the order to launch the ships into the sea, Odysseus prevented him by pointing out that that was the surest way to start a panic in the Greek army, and all would be lost.[3] Instead, the order was given to stand firm: there must be no further retreat. And when Hector reached the line of ships, great Ajax was there with his gigantic shield, like a mighty rock against which the waves hurl their fury in vain.

The tide of the Trojan onslaught had already begun to ebb when at last Achilles came forth fresh and shining in new armour to smite the enemy and send them reeling back to Troy. With the Trojans fleeing before the wrath of Achilles and his Myrmidons it was now Hector's turn to panic. The enemy commander fled, and the Greek champion chased him three times round the walls of Troy before, exhausted, he turned at bay and was felled by a blow from Achilles' lance.

With the death of Hector, the Trojans' hope of hurling the Greeks back into the sea was ended. Their army was now cooped up in the city. But the Greeks were still far from their objective - the re-capture of Helen, immured in the Trojan citadel - for the walls of Troy were now fortified and defended more strongly than ever. And when, soon after, Achilles himself died from a wound received when Paris shot him in the heel with an arrow, the last Greek hope of victory vanished.

After nine years of fighting, the Greek troops were exhausted and demoralised. There were numerous mutinies and desertions. Wasted by fighting and disease and starved of supplies they were desperately short of manpower, food and weapons. Nor was there any hope of more help coming from home. The economy of Argos and some other states was on the verge of collapse; Achaea was in the hands of a government which was opposed to the war and refused to send any more re-inforcements. Not one state was either able or willing to make any further effort. The whole of Europe was exhausted.

The Greek leaders met in a final council. Agamemnon, haunted by the memory of Iphigeneia and afraid to face his wife empty-handed of victory, had already postponed the inevitable decision till the end of the summer. Soon the autumn winds would begin to blow and it would be too dangerous for sailing. But at last he could delay no longer. He was forced to admit defeat. The council met in gloomy silence. There was no hope - only blank despair. Behind them were the memories of the flower of European manhood perished, and the stored-up wealth of centuries of patient industry squandered in vain. In front of them was a nightmare: the return home to face the reproaches of their wives and their peoples and to be remembered for ever as the men who had brought their civilization to ruin.

For Western civilization had reached the end of the road.

Western supremacy was finished. The West had thrown all it had into the struggle. The mightiest force ever assembled on earth had been hurled against the walls of Troy, and the walls still stood. Never before had so humiliating a defeat been suffered on so vast a scale. The East had triumphed. Asia and Africa - for African troops under Memnon fought on the Trojan side - had roused themselves and by a mighty effort shaken off the age-old yoke of European domination. The future that now lay before them was a future bright with promise.

The day was fixed for the Greeks' departure and the order given for the ships to be made ready. There was a great deal to be done. Many of them were no longer seaworthy. Their timbers had rotted, the metal parts were corroded and the rigging perished. But a sufficient number was in a good enough condition to be repaired and fitted out to carry the shrunken force back to their home ports.

Odysseus, always in demand when technical difficulties arose, was never more busily occupied than in these last few days. Shipwrights, riggers and quartermasters from all the contingents sought his advice on their problems. He passed up and down the beach inspecting the ships and their gear, enquiring into difficulties and suggesting solutions. When presented with a problem he examined it carefully in detail and would often spot a feature which the experts had overlooked and which pointed the way to a solution. If need be he would not hesitate to take the tools in his own hands and demonstrate how they could be used. All the men knew him, and none came to him without receiving a sensible and often ingenious answer to his problem.

Two days before the fleet was due to sail, Odysseus was returning, late in the evening, to his tent, worn out with the day's toil. As he was about to leave the beach he noticed a ship, apparently in good condition, still drawn up on the shore. All other seaworthy vessels were already in the water, and the rest were being broken up, stripped of all serviceable fittings, and burned. A number of men were gathered round arguing about whether the ship should be launched or not. Odysseus stopped and asked what was the matter.

"The timbers are a bit rotten, Sir," came the reply.

"She looks all right to me," said Odysseus, prodding the side with the point of his sword. "Where's the trouble?"

"In here, Sir," said the man, and led the way over the side and into the hold under the stern deck. It was dark inside, but Odysseus could feel where the wood was soft and spongy. It was a flat bottomed boat, with no keel. He gave his opinion that the bottom would not stand up to the strain of a moderate sea.

"Then we'd better set her alight, Sir," the man said.

"I suppose you'd better," he answered as they climbed out. But before leaving he changed his mind. "Wait," he said, "She may be useful for something yet. Leave her till tomorrow."

"Very good, Sir."

Odysseus could think of no purpose for which an unseaworthy ship might conceivably be useful, but it was his instinct never to destroy anything until it was necessary to do so. As he left the beach he turned and took a last look at the vessel silhouetted against the darkening sky.

"What's her name?" he called out.

"We call her The Wooden Horse", came the reply.

Notes on Chapter 6 - The Scapegoat

1. Homer's somewhat different and much longer account of this episode is contained in the tenth book of the *Iliad*, known as the *Doloneia*. The authorship of that book has been called in question in both ancient and modern times. Scholars have attacked it as being out of tune with the rest of the *Iliad* and inferior in the quality of its poetry; and its subject-matter, its style, and its language have been condemned as 'un-Homeric'. These criticisms were examined in detail line by line, by Alexander Shewan in a scholarly book, *The Lay of Dolon* (Macmillan 1911), in which he showed that none of them was well-founded. The tenth book, he concluded, in all respects was 'all of a piece' with the rest of the *Iliad*.

Shewan's philological analysis incidentally corroborated the verdict that had been pronounced earlier on aesthetic grounds by the philosopher-poet Goethe: namely that the *Iliad* and the *Odyssey* were creations of the same poetic genius. The ancients had never doubted that Homer was the author of both epics, but some modern commentators had expressed doubts on account of the differences in their subject-matter and in their attitudes towards the gods. These differences can be accounted for by the explanation I put forward in this chapter. The *Doloneia* is the link between the two poems, indicating as it does the probability that the basic material for both emanated from the same original source, namely the mind of Odysseus, King of Ithaca.

In telling the story of his adventurous life to his children and grandchildren in his old age Odysseus did not reveal how he had tricked Diomede out of his prize at the games for the throne of Sparta, nor did he give any hint that he and Diomede were other than friendly companions when they set off on their night errand of espionage.

He reckoned on being able to fill in those gaps in the record on some future occasion after his death. Those experiences were such that not all the waters of Lethe would be able to wash away their memories.

2. *Iliad* 11. 373-488.
3. *Iliad* 14. 82-102.

Chapter 7
THE WOODEN HORSE

That night, while Odysseus slept, the cells in his brain were working busily. He awoke in the morning with a start. Side by side before his mind's eye were two pictures, both of which were associated with the feel and smell of damp rotting wood. The first was a picture of the dark interior of the ship's hold he had just inspected. The second was the dark interior of a disused pigsty he had once hidden in, years before when he was a boy in his native Ithaca.

Odysseus was the younger of two sons of whom the elder died young. A bright boy, Odysseus was quick at finding and making new toys to play with, but his older brother was jealous and would try to snatch his toys away and break them. Once, after seeing a cartwheel come off its axle and go rolling downhill on its own, Odysseus made himself a hoop out of willow twigs, which he bowled along, guiding it with a stick. But his big brother chased him, seized the hoop, and ran off with it down the hill.

Odysseus gave chase, but the boy ran to an old farm shed at the foot of the hill, threw the hoop inside, shut the door and then stood on guard outside to bar his entry. When verbal appeals failed to move the boy, Odysseus attacked him, and tried to pull him away to get at the door behind him. But the boy was too strong and his position too secure. After many fruitless attempts to dislodge him, Odysseus had to give up. Frustrated and angry he walked slowly back up the hill in the direction of his father's house.

On the way he met a shepherd who greeted him respectfully. He did not answer. A few steps further he paused for breath and looked back. The shepherd was following the path that ran past the shed, now hidden from him by the corner of a wood. He had an idea. Striking off the path at right angles he ran for some distance, crouching with his head down to keep out of sight, then turned again at right angles and doubled back on a route parallel to the way he had come. Passing behind the back of the shed he stole quietly up on the other side and hid there in an old pigsty that leaned up against the wall.

Presently the shepherd came by. As Odysseus had expected, his brother hailed the shepherd and asked if he had seen Odysseus.

"Yes," said the man. "I passed him just now. He was on his way home."

The boy at once relaxed his guard and left his post by the door to see for himself. While his back was turned, Odysseus crept out from his hiding place and with a cry of triumph established himself in the other's stronghold, barring the door.

The two boys' roles were now reversed. But Odysseus was defending what was his own and the other had no heart for a struggle to steal the hoop a second time. After a brief struggle he gave up, and Odysseus carried the prize home in triumph.

As he lay awake in his tent on the plain of Troy it now seemed to him that that incident was both symbolic and purposeful. He felt as if it had happened for the express purpose of putting into his head a plan for the capture of the Trojan citadel. It did not take him long to work one out, following the pattern of his boyhood victory. He got up quickly and ran straight to the tent of Diomede and explained his plan. Diomede was enthusiastic and the two went together and persuaded Agamemnon to call a hurried meeting of the war council.

Odysseus addressed the council with a new assurance and in a tone of command, as if he were himself the commander-in-chief. He was propounding a plan for the capture of the enemy citadel, and that, he had decided, was a matter that was too important to be left in the hands of the legitimate authorities. They had made a muddle of the campaign up to now. They had had their opportunity, and they had failed. They must not be allowed to bungle the only feasible plan for final victory.

The plan, he explained, was in two parts. The first was for the whole fleet to put to sea, as arranged, on the following afternoon and sail away to the west. At a certain time, depending on the wind, one squadron would turn round, and sail back, disembarking on the beach in time to be able to reach the Dardanian gate by moonrise at 4 am. He proposed that this part of the plan be under the command of Agamemnon and Nestor, to whom would be attached the best navigator in the fleet to guide them.

The second part was for twelve picked leaders to conceal themselves in the *Wooden Horse* which would be drawn overland and left outside the gate as a sacrifice to Poseidon. That god, he pointed out, was both the god of the sea and the reputed founder-deity of Troy. The *Wooden Horse* was an ordinary flat-bottomed ship, hollow in the middle, and with short decks at either end under which were holds used for the storage of food, water and equipment. There was room for about six lightly armed men in each hold. A man, preferably a priest, would stay with the ship to explain its purpose to the Trojans and to give warning by signal to the men inside in the event of any untoward occurrence.

Odysseus hoped that, with reasonable luck, the Trojans might actually pull the ship in through the gates that evening, but if they left it outside the men would scale the wall with a ladder which would be left hidden for the purpose. There would be no guard awake on the wall that night, he was sure, for after they had seen the Greek fleet depart the Trojans would be far too busy celebrating to bother any more about their defences. There would not be a sober man in Troy that night.

When the main force reached the gate they were to throw a stone over the wall. That would be the signal for the men inside to open the gates, having overcome any resistance that might be offered by the sentries. Odysseus let it be assumed that he himself would direct the party in the ship and would allocate them their duties separately.

The plan was adopted and the council broke up in excitement, each leader hurrying off to prepare for his part in the operation. The news ran through the army like an electric shock. Suddenly in the place of black despair there was hope. "Odysseus has a plan!" "Odysseus is in command!" As the words flashed from mouth to mouth the spectre of defeat was transformed into a radiant vision of victory; for there was scarcely a man in the whole Greek host who did not believe that Odysseus was the favourite of Pallas Athene, and that if he devised a plan and were charged to put it into execution, that plan would succeed.

The popular belief that Odysseus was beloved by the goddess Athene sprang not so much from his reputation as a peace-maker before the war or as a problem-solver during it as from the episode of his night operation with Diomede. Everyone knew that the merciless King of Argos had sworn vengeance on him for his part in the contest for Helen's hand, so when Diomede chose Odysseus to accompany him that night no-one expected to see him alive again. Therefore when he returned not only alive but arm-in-arm, so to speak, with his would-be murderer they could scarcely believe their eyes. It was as if they were looking at a dead man who had risen from the grave. There could be no doubt that some divine power had preserved him. That same power would now surely give them victory.

The day was spent in feverish preparation. By the following afternoon all was ready. The *Wooden Horse* was floated onto an improvised trolley made from unwanted chariots, drawn by horses up to the city and left, with its secret cargo of armed men, outside the Dardanian gate. Then the fleet put to sea, and the whole of Troy came out onto the city walls and rejoiced as they watched the hated ships sail away out of sight. But there were many widows and fatherless for whom there was little comfort. Most disconsolate of all was Helen whose beloved Paris had been killed at the very end of the fighting and who now faced the prospect of living into old age in a foreign country alone with her guilty memories.

The sight of the *Wooden Horse* outside the gate aroused some speculation, but no undue suspicion. It seemed reasonable enough that the Greeks should want to propitiate the seagod in this way before their dangerous voyage home. Anyway, the Trojans were in no mood to be critical. They pulled the ship into the city, set it in front of the Temple of Poseidon and danced round it in celebration of their victory.

The revelry lasted far into the night. When at last all was quiet, Odysseus and his men stole from their hiding place and made for the gate. There was no need to overpower the drunken sentries. They waited in silence. As the moon rose, the stillness was broken by the sound of a stone falling on the roadway. The army had arrived. The gates were thrown open and the Greek host entered the citadel of Troy.

Odysseus, Diomede and Menelaus made straight for the palace and captured Helen. Then, while Menelaus carried her to safety, the other two seized the Palladion, the sacred image of Athene which was the symbol of Trojan sovereignty, and carried it out of the citadel.

Now began a terrible holocaust. Fire was set to the houses on the perimeter, and as the flames spread inwards the terrified people rushed screaming into the streets, to be cut to pieces by the pitiless Greek soldiery. Prayers and entreaties availed them nothing. No one was spared. Men, women and children alike were burned or butchered without mercy. Those who sought refuge in the temples were dragged out to be slaughtered or were cut down on the spot as they clung to the altars of the gods. Among them were old Priam himself and his queen Hecuba. The entire population of Troy was done to death. Scarcely one man escaped.

By the end of the next day the great city that had once proudly dominated the Dardanelles was nothing but a smoking ruin. The West had gained the victory at last.

Chapter 8
A TALK BY THE SEA

"Let me die! Let me die! I won't go back. I won't. It's all my fault. I want to die."

Helen was hysterical. Appalled by the horror of the burning city and afraid to return to Greece and face the reproaches of the people on whom she had brought untold miseries, she was trying to drown herself in the sea. But Menelaus and Odysseus swam after her and their strong arms dragged her ashore. After a while she ceased to struggle and lay on the sand, sobbing. Her husband tried to soothe her, but it was to Odysseus that she turned for comfort.

"I'll talk to her awhile," he said to his companion. "She'll be better presently." And Menelaus, glad of the opportunity to disengage himself, went off to attend to the preparations for his departure. The rest of the army had already left, and these two were the last of the Greek captains to go, having been delayed by Helen's refusal to return with her husband to Sparta.

"It's all my fault. Why won't you let me die?" she kept repeating. "Let me end this agony."

"It wasn't all your fault," answered Odysseus. There were lots of other people who must share the blame for the war. In fact, I was partly to blame myself."

"You? How?"

"Do you remember the time when Menelaus and I came to try to persuade you to come home? We spoke to the King in council, and then addressed a meeting of the people. Well, I heard afterwards that if I had not spoken as I did to the people Priam would have let you go. It was because I had made my warning public that he felt obliged to keep you, in order not to lose face with his people. I did not know then that oriental people set so much store by saving face. I thought they were more intelligent. A sensible man doesn't risk death to save his face, much less does he endanger the lives of all his people for what he chooses to call their national prestige. But Priam and Hector were not sensible. Their pride was stronger than their intelligence, and the Trojan people were too servile to insist on their government doing the right and sensible thing after Menelaus and I had warned them of the consequences of not letting you go. Those were the primary causes of the war as I see it - Priam's pride and his people's servility. The offer you made to go back with us to Sparta seems to me to absolve you from all responsibility for what happened after that."

"Thank you," said Helen. "That makes me feel a lot better. But aren't you being rather hard on Priam and Hector? They could not possibly have known it was going to be such a ghastly war and that we were going to lose it in the end. In fact, we very nearly won. The citadel was really impregnable. You would never have succeeded in getting inside if it hadn't been for that dirty rotten trick you played, hiding in that old ship."

"The Wooden Horse?"

"Was that what it was called? What a funny name for a ship."

"It wasn't its real name. The men called it that because of the way it behaved on the sea. Its real name was Pegasus, the Flying Horse. A 'wooden horse', you know, is the child's toy that most people nowadays call a 'rocking-horse'. It was one of the special ships that had been built under emergency measures by a firm that normally made crates. It was shaped like a crate too, only with the ends sloping upwards. You can imagine what it was like on the sea - very good at going up and down and very bad at going forward - just like a rocking-horse."

Helen laughed. She had recovered her composure now and was sitting up, tidying her hair.

"I suppose," he went on, "you think it wrong for soldiers to play what you call 'dirty tricks' in war, don't you? One ought to fight battles according to strict rules, all straight-forward, honest and above-board. Like a boxing match. No hitting below the belt on pain of being disqualified. In that case, of course, the strongest side would always win and there would be no scope for more than a very limited amount of intelligence - as in boxing. Well, that's not the way it is. Fortunately for mankind, war is more like a wrestling match with no holds barred."

"Why fortunately for mankind?"

"Because man's progress depends on the evolution of his intelligence, and therefore in every struggle for survival it is essential that the victory should go to the most intelligent. It's the only way to salvation."

"What do you mean by 'salvation'?"

"I mean the time when man will be the intelligent master of himself as well as of his surroundings, when war and strife will have been abolished and all people will live in peace and harmony with one another and with nature."

"You don't really believe that time will ever come, do you?"

"It's bound to, for two reasons. In the first place, as I have said, in the course of the struggles for survival which we call history, superior intelligence will win in the end. An army composed of men well-endowed with commonsense, initiative, and guts, equipped with advanced weaponry, and commanded by clever generals will always defeat one that relies solely on strength of numbers."

"But surely that is just what the Greeks were doing - relying on strength of numbers and nothing else. I remember Hector saying how badly organised the Greek army was, and that was why they would never win."

"He was right. We never could have won the way we were fighting then. Our army was badly organised because it wasn't one army but a collection of armies under independent sovereign kings. It was only at the very end, after Agamemnon had admitted defeat, that we got ourselves properly organised for the final assault - what you called that 'dirty trick'. That proves my point. It was not force of numbers that won the war but an idea, an intelligent plan.

"There is a second and more important reason why I look forward to the ultimate abolition of war, and the substitution of the rule of intelligence for the rule of force. This is that history itself is being guided by a Higher Intelligence that is working and planning to bring that about. How do I know that? Because many strange events have happened in my life. More than once I have felt myself impelled by a Power that was stronger than myself, driving me on to a destiny that was planned for me from the beginning. It is an intelligent Power, and I call it Pallas Athene. I hated the thought of war and did not want to come to Troy, but Athene drove me here against my will. I succumbed to her and obeyed her summons, and she protected me miraculously when I was in danger of being killed." Here he recounted the story of his night raid with Diomede. "And finally she inspired me with that idea of the Wooden Horse. I hated the fire and the slaughter. It was horrible, horrible. But it had to happen. That was how it had been planned. It was the same last time."

"Last time, what do you mean? There's never been anything like this before."

"Not exactly like it. This time it was fire and sword; last time it was water. I warned them then as I warned them this time, but they would not listen. It was their own fault, and when they realised their fate, it was too late. If only they had listened."

"Please explain. What are you talking about?"

"Have you ever had the feeling that this had all happened before?"

"Yes, sometimes quite clearly."

"When you feel that, it is because an echo has been aroused in your subconscious memory - an echo of something that happened to you in a former life. You see, we have not one life only, but many. Perhaps an infinite number. The memories of all past lives are buried below the surface of your conscious mind and influence you as instincts. They warn you to keep away from dangers that caused you harm and they attract you to things that gave you pleasure. It follows that, as life succeeds life, each of us learns by his experiences and behaves instinctively, if not from conscious reasoning, in an increasingly intelligent manner, provided we always suffer from our folly and neglect, and profit from our wisdom and industry."

"What if we do not?"

"We are bound to in the end, because justice is absolute and eternal and no man can escape it for ever. It is inherent in the nature of the universe."

Helen looked at him uncomprehendingly.

"You see," he went on, "I know I have lived before, and will live again, because I can remember my former life. It has come back to me quite clearly over the last few days, since the sack of the citadel. When all those terrified people were screaming and begging for mercy, I had the feeling: this had all happened before. Then it all began to come back. Bit by bit the memory pieced itself together in my brain. I made no effort. The ideas just floated up into my consciousness, and I found I knew things which I had not known before. And yet I felt that I had known them all my life. Shall I tell you?"

"Yes, please do."

"Let us take a walk up on the cliffs."

There, walking slowly with his eyes fixed on the ground in front of him, Odysseus began the story of his former life.

Chapter 9
A MARK ON A WALL

"I lived in a city in the centre of a plain through which flowed a river. It was an immense river, like the Nile, only it was not the Nile because it was contained between two high embankments and its surface was above the level of the surrounding plain. It was navigated by many ships, being the principal means of transport for the territory.

"I was an engineer employed by the government. By hard work and application I rose to become the Chief Engineer of the realm, with special responsibility for engineering works on the river. But mine was not the chief responsibility. That rested with the Minister of Works, an important noble who was not an engineer himself, but whose duty it was to decide the policy and instruct me what to do.

"My first Minister was a very energetic man and he earned for himself a reputation for great efficiency by improving the transport system, building new jetties and wharves and in many other ways facilitating the flow of trade and commerce. It was a wealthy country and merchants were very powerful. My Minister was popular with them, and I had to work very hard to carry out the numerous projects which he approved for their accommodation and enrichment.

"In due course this Minister died and was replaced by another, a lazy man who did not like to be disturbed. He, too, knew nothing about engineering. He left me to run the Works Department largely as I wished.

"For a long time I had been uneasy about the state of the river. It did not seem to me natural that a river should flow above the level of the plain. But no-one else thought it odd, and everybody assumed it had been like that for ever. There was no recollection of it ever having been otherwise. And yet I was certain that those embankments had been made by human hands. When, why, how, I could not tell.

"Taking advantage of my new freedom, I made a thorough survey of the waterway. At one point where it flowed past the city, some buildings had been built right into the embankment, and the water was contained by a vertical stone wall - or it may have been a brick wall, I do not remember. What I do remember is that I noticed a mark on this wall: a faint mark, almost obliterated by age. It had clearly been put there for a purpose, but I could not tell what it signified. My curiosity was aroused and I wanted to find out.

"I asked everyone who I thought might know, but no one could tell me what it meant. Scarcely anyone had even noticed it. The oldest fisherman on the river said it had been there all his life. Then I searched through the records. My predecessors for generations back had been scrupulous in keeping records of everything they had done, and these records were all carefully preserved in the archives of the Works Department. I got them out and went through them methodically. It was a laborious task. At length I came to the entry I was looking for. It related to an event that had occurred a long time, perhaps two or three hundred years, before - I do not remember.

"The entry recorded that after very heavy rains the river had reached a flood level higher than had ever been recorded before. It came almost to the top of the embankments, but it did not overflow. There must have been a great scare, because after it went down the embankments were raised to a higher level to give a new margin of safety. The entry described the mark which had been made on the wall to record the flood level, and it gave the depth of the water in the centre of the river at that point.

"Now the mark I had noticed tallied with the description,

74

but it was no longer high above the water level. It was regularly submerged when the river was in spate. I hastened to take measurements, and found by calculation that the bed of the river was now some feet higher than it had been when the record was made. I saw at last what was happening. The river was silting up. It had been silting up for hundreds of years. By a further calculation I reckoned that, given another wet spring and the same amount of water in the river as had caused the earlier record, the level this time would come well over the top of the embankment. And I was sure that if that happened, the banks would be destroyed and the whole land would be flooded.

"There was only one thing to do: to raise the banks still higher, and then undertake a systematic dredging operation to deepen the channel. I sat down and worked out a plan. It was a practical plan which would have saved the country, but it was very costly. It involved enlisting the entire manpower of the nation as an emergency measure for work along the whole length of the embankments - some hundreds of miles. When I had worked it out, I presented a comprehensive report to the Minister describing the danger of a flood and my recommen-dations for dealing with it.

"At first the Minister refused to believe my conclusion. He made light of the mark on the wall, refused to examine the records, and was unable to follow the calculations. He had never heard of a river silting up. The idea was new to him and he could not grasp it. There was no word meaning 'silt' in the language. No flood had ever happened in the past and he saw no reason to suppose that one would happen in the future. The whole idea was fantastic. Obviously I had made a mistake. Even if I was right about the danger, my plan for dealing with it was unrealistic. The Treasury, he said, would not even look at it.

"When I heard that my report had been rejected, I decided to make it public. Disobeying the rules of my service, I called a meeting of the people and addressed them in the market-place. I said their lives were in danger, and I told them what I had proposed should be done to save the country from extinction. I gave them the figures and invited them to check the calculations for themselves.

"These words coming from the Chief Engineer carried weight with the people and filled them with alarm. The Minister was very angry. He dismissed me from the service and appointed in my place one of my subordinates who showed more respect for his superiors. To meet the public alarm the Minister was forced to re-examine my report, and he consulted this man for fresh technical advice.

"Desiring to please both the Minister and the Treasury, the new Chief Engineer said he doubted my conclusions about the danger, and suggested that what danger there was could be met by less far-reaching measures. He pooh-poohed the idea that the embankments might give way, and he put forward a compromise plan for raising them by only a small amount in the neighbourhood of the city only, to meet the possibility of a slight overflow there.

The government were pleased with this inexpensive proposal and decided to adopt it.

"The public were calmed by official spokesmen who assured them there was no immediate danger, that the government had the situation well in hand and would take all measures necessary for the people's safety. My report was condemned as false and alarmist. I was described as a mere technician who had failed to understand the wider political and economic aspects of a complex problem. The most telling point against me, which they emphasised, was that I was alone in my view. No one, even in my own department, supported me, either because they did not understand as I did or, if they did, because they feared to lose their jobs if they spoke up.

"The people's fear which I had aroused then turned to anger and was vented in hatred against me. I was spat upon and insulted in the streets and rude signs were scribbled on my door. So I left the city and bought a farm. I was still convinced that the flood was going to come and I kept wondering what could be done.

"Then one day I had an idea. I remembered an incident that had happened when I was a boy. It was when I was about ten years old. I was sitting by the pond in my home village, putting the finishing touches to a model farmyard which I had fashioned out of mud on a slab of stone, when my elder brother came by, saw what I was doing, seized the slab and threw it into the pond. When I picked it out, all the buildings I had modelled in mud had been washed away, but the farmhouse itself, which I had made from a block of wood, was floating intact on the surface of the water, and I was able to rescue it.

"It now seemed to me that that incident was both symbolic and purposeful. It was as if it had been intentionally designed to show me how I could save myself and my family from the coming deluge. I decided to build a wooden house on a raft in such a way that it would float intact on the surface of the water when the flood came. I had begun my engineering career as a shipwright and I knew how to apply the techniques of boat-building to the building of a water-proof ark. I calculated the dimensions to ensure that it would float correctly, and then set about building it, with the help of my family. I showed other people what I was doing and urged them to follow my example. But they only laughed at me. They said I was a crank and my ark became a favourite butt for their jokes.

"No sooner was the ark finished than the rains came, the river overflowed, the embankments gave way, and the whole country was inundated. The waters swirled round the ark and lifted it up off the ground, with me and my family of children and grandchildren safe inside the house and my farm animals on the outer parts of the raft. But all other houses were destroyed. The water was full of a terrified mass of people screaming for help. As the ark floated towards the city, hundreds of people struggled to reach it and tried to scramble on board. But there was no room for them. They had had their chance to save themselves and had not taken it. It was too late now. My sons and I stood on the edge of the raft and pushed them off with poles. The kindest thing we could do was to hold their heads under the water until they drowned. Men, women and children. Even the babies were drowned. They were their parents' responsibility. It was horrible, horrible.

"If only they had followed my advice while there was yet time. I had warned them and set them an example. What more could I have done? If only they had heeded my warning! If only they had followed my example! They might all have been saved. But they preferred to obey their government. The government had the legal responsibility. They were the financiers and the politicians; they had the power. I was only the engineer; I only had the knowledge. I could only warn them, and show them the way. I could not compel them to follow.

"I was rejected by the government and reviled by the people. When it all happened as I predicted, what was the use of their coming to me and imploring me to save them? It was too late. They had made their decisions, and they had to take the consequences.

"Then the ark was carried away from the city and out over where the forests had been. There the water was full of struggling animals. For them I had compassion, for they had had no chance to save themselves. We picked as many different varieties as we could out of the water, a male and a female of each, and put them on the raft with the farm animals.

"I steered the ark so that when the waters receded it grounded on the top of a hill, which was now an island. And there I started afresh to build a new world."

Chapter 10
EASTERN QUEST

When Odysseus had finished his story, there was a long silence broken only by the murmur of the waves breaking on the rocks below. For the first time in her life, Helen could think of nothing to say.

At length she asked, half incredulously: "Do you really remember all that?"

"I remember the principles, the general ideas, clearly," he answered. "The details I filled in from my imagination. I did not remember the whole story all at once. The main events came back one by one and I fitted them together by inference. When the story was complete I knew that that was how it had happened because it all made sense. It had to happen like that. There was something inevitable about it, just as there was about this war."

"Were you very excited when you remembered?"

"Not at all. No emotion of any kind accompanied the recollection. It all seemed familiar, as if I had known it all my life. Imagine yourself to be sitting alone in a room at night, with one dim candle burning by which you can see a few objects close at hand. Those objects are the events of your present life. Then the dawn comes and the whole room gradually becomes light. One by one you pick out the outlines of more distant objects, and you know what they are because you put them there yourself. The room is familiar, because it is your own room, and it is furnished the way you furnished it yourself, with the deeds of your former lives. That is how I have felt in these last few days - as if a new day had dawned, enabling me to see clearly many things that were hidden from me before."

He paused.

"The curious thing is," he went on, "that the events that I remember about that flood do not tally with any actual events that I have ever heard of. The Greek flood from which Deucalion was saved must have been quite different because there is no river in Greece like the one I remember. Have you, since you came to Troy, heard of any story resembling mine?"

"Yes," answered Helen, "I have. It reminds me of a tale I heard told by a traveller from the east about a man called Noah."

"What river was it?"

"I don't remember there being a river in the story, but the man who told it came from somewhere near the Euphrates."

"I must go there," said Odysseus, "and find out all I can about that flood."

"Why?"

"Because I have got to prove to myself beyond any possibility of doubt that I have lived before. The story I have told you could be a kind of waking dream, a hallucination of a fevered brain. But if it fits into a pattern of historical events of which I was ignorant, that will constitute for me proof that my recollection is a genuine memory of a former life. I cannot rest until I have proved that memory either right or wrong."

"Suppose you prove it right, what will you do then?"

"When I have proved it to myself I shall have to set about proving it to others."

"How will you do that?"

"I don't know yet. I'll have to find a way. It will be important because it should make a big difference to many people if reincarnation can be established as a proven fact and not just a religious belief. Would you and Paris, for instance, have run off in the way you did if you had known for certain that you would be held to account in a future life?"

"I don't know. I just acted on an impulse. I didn't stop to think about the consequences for this life, let alone the next. I can't answer for poor dear Paris. He has paid for it with his life now. I still wish you would let me do the same."

"Suicide is not the same as being killed in battle. In your case it would simply be a way of escape, and an unsuccessful one at that."

"How do you mean?"

"If Nemesis works in the way I think she should, then if you did wrong when you eloped - and I emphasise the word 'if' because I don't want you to think I'm judging you - if in your judgement you did wrong, then sooner or later you will have to pay. You can't escape the consequences for ever. As I see it, if you are sorry for what you did, and you now return with your husband to Sparta and brave the insults which the women there will heap on you, you will be given an opportunity in a future life to redeem yourself."

Helen argued no more. She laid her head on his shoulder and sobbed quietly. Odysseus enfolded her lovingly in his arms and held her until she stopped crying, and he felt at last she was at peace.

Helen returned to Greece with Menelaus and resumed her position as Queen of Sparta. Such was her charm and beauty and so evident her sorrow and self-reproach that the people forgave her. She did not have to suffer the insults she had expected, but reigned in quiet contentment for the rest of her life, enjoying the substance and privileges of her position.

While Menelaus and Helen were setting sail on their way home to the west, Odysseus was making preparations for a longer sojourn in the east. Much as he longed after ten years of war to be home with his family in peaceful Ithaca, he obeyed what he deemed to be the call of a higher duty, turned his back on Greece, and sailed south and east round the coast of Asia Minor in a quest for knowledge.

He disembarked at the mouth of the Orontes, and thence travelled overland through Alalakh and Aleppo to the upper reaches of the Euphrates, asking questions as he journeyed and picking up many tales of far-off times.

He heard many versions of the story of Noah, or, as some called him, Ut-na-pishtim. They differed in details but they all agreed in their account of how, on divine instructions, a man built an ark and saved himself, his family, and many animals, from the Flood. Odysseus was certain that that man was indeed himself. But he was puzzled by the absence of any reference to the overflowing of the river as he remembered it. And there were a number of points in the traditional stories which in his view were manifestly impossible. No flood could possibly have reached the top of Mount Ararat, nor was it within the bounds of reasonable probability that, in a normally arid region, seven or eight inches of rain per day would fall for forty consecutive days. Odysseus concluded that his memory of the events of many centuries ago was more accurate than the history handed down by the poets. But he was not yet satisfied. He journeyed by boat down the whole length of the Euphrates without finding any trace of the high embankments he had expected to find. He questioned many people but no one could remember any stories of the river ever having been different from what it was. At last he reached the mouth and, still unsatisfied, took a passage on board a merchantman bound for Suez.

It was when the ship reached the island of Bahrein, and the skipper remarked that that was where the ark was supposed to have grounded, that the truth was revealed to Odysseus. By examining the charts and taking soundings of the shallow sea as they proceeded further down the coast, he confirmed his idea. Without doubt here, under the water, lay his former abode. There must, he reckoned, have been a rise in the sea-level, or a sinking of the land level, which had necessitated the building and periodic raising of embankments to contain the river, and of dykes across the Strait of Hormuz to keep out the sea. The failure of these defences caused by the silting up and over-flowing of the river not only provided a satisfactory explanation of the colossal scale of the Flood - a feature on which all accounts were agreed - but it also cleared up the mystery which had puzzled him for so long: his memory of the mark on the wall.

That memory was confirmed for him unequivocally by the description, given in more than one version of the Flood story, of the medium through which Noah received the divine instruction to build his ark. It was Ea, the god of Mind, who instructed the hero *through a wall*, and so outwitted Enlil, the god of Matter. [1]

Odysseus' far memory of that mark on a wall not only explained for him the meaning of Ea's message; it also told him why the record of the message had come down through the centuries in that enigmatic form. It was because he himself, as Noah, had told the story in that way as a kind of experiment designed to enable him to identify himself in a later incarnation. For who else but a former river engineer like himself who knew that reliable predictions of coming floods or other such physical events are made not by interpreting dreams or listening to mystic voices in one's head but by taking measurements and making calculations - who else would be likely to solve the riddle contained in that message?

But whilst Noah's experiment had been successful in con-vincing his future self, Odysseus, of his identity, it was useless for his now more important purpose of enabling him to convince others. Sheer physical distance placed an insuperable barrier in the way. The Greeks had never heard of Noah, and the Babylonians had never heard of Odysseus. His idea of using his memory to establish the reality of reincarnation for the world at large would therefore have to wait for a later age when civilization should have expanded so as to encompass a wider area of the globe. His immediate task was to repeat his former experiment and devise a means of passing another enigmatic message for himself across the centuries to come, such as would enable him then to establish his identity to the satisfaction not of himself alone but this time of others also.

With these thoughts in mind Odysseus at last turned his face towards home. But he did not reach Ithaca without further incident. On the last stage of his journey his ship was wrecked on the rocky coast and he was nearly drowned. Swimming through mountainous waves he just reached the shore as his strength was exhausted. A kindly swineherd found him and cared for him not knowing who he was. Clothed in rags he entered his palace to find that his faithful wife Penelope had at last lost hope of his ever coming back and was preparing to marry again. The house was full of young men suing for her hand, spurred on by the prospect of obtaining the Kingdom of Ithaca as a dowry. According to custom, an athletic contest was to be held to decide the issue.

Odysseus was recognised first by his old nurse Eurycleia. Then he revealed himself to his son Telemachus and to some trusted members of his staff. Finally, when he was assured of sufficient support, he made himself known to Penelope, and sent the suitors packing.

When he had put the affairs of his kingdom in order, he settled down to carry out a plan that he had formulated on his way home. He wrote a record of the history of the Trojan War, from Paris's abduction of Helen to the sack of the citadel. He recounted the details of the forces engaged on either side and described many of the incidents which occur in the Iliad. But certain significant details of incidents in which he had been personally concerned he omitted: the reason for his quarrel with Achilles, Diomede's intent to murder him in the night, and how he conceived the idea for the Wooden Horse stratagem. He reckoned that in his next life he would be able to fill in these gaps in the record and, by turning an improbable story into one more likely to be true, to convince other people that he had lived before.

But when the record was finished, Odysseus was not satisfied. Even if his plan worked out as he hoped, would many people be convinced? Would they not say he had invented those parts of the stories which he said he remembered? Would it not be just as impossible for him then to prove his account of the Wooden Horse as it was now to prove his account of the Flood? Both accounts could have been pure fiction. Perhaps other rationalisations, no less credible than his own, would be advanced by others. Who would then believe him?

Proof of veracity is a question of mathematical probabilities. To prove the truth of a proposition, the greater its apparent improbability the greater must be the improbability of the supporting evidence being false. Modern skeptics hold it to be improbable in the extreme that a man once dead can return to life. Odysseus was not yet satisfied that the evidence he would be able in his next life to adduce by way of proof would be strong enough to overcome their disbelief.

So he continued to wrestle with his problem, until he was struck by a new idea. A much better idea. This time he was satisfied that he had found a way by which he would be able to provide convincing, if not conclusive, proof, in his next life that he, Odysseus, son of Laertes, had returned to live again. It happened like this.

It was bedtime for his little granddaughter, and she was sitting on his knee begging him to tell her one of the tales of his adventures in foreign lands, before her mother came to tuck her up for the night.

"Shall I tell you the story of how I conquered the Kikons?" he said.

"The what?" she asked.

"The Kikons."

"Oh, do you know what I thought you said, Grandpapa?"

"No, what?"

"I thought you said: 'Shall I tell you how I conquered the hiccups'! Wasn't that funny?"

Grandpapa thought it very funny and they laughed together. But when he thought about it again later it struck him as significant. The Kikons were a Thracian people belonging to the kingdom on the Gallipoli peninsular with which Hector had negotiated a political union before the war. Early in the war Odysseus had proposed an expedition against them with the double objective of knocking out one of the Trojan dependencies and securing a good source of food supply for the Greek army. Kikonia was rich in corn and wine, and many of the Greek contingents were far from adequately fed.

The proposal was approved and Odysseus led the expe-dition, which was successful. But his men ate and drank so well after their victory that he had difficulty in getting them away in good order. It now struck him as an odd coincidence that the name 'Kikons' was similar to the word used by the little girl to mean 'hiccups'. For to say that, when he had succeeded in getting his drunken soldiers under control, ' he had conquered the hiccups' was not, after all, so very far from the truth.

This was the germ of the idea that now began to develop in his mind. His life had been full of adventures. He had had many struggles, both with other men and with the forces of nature, from all of which after many setbacks he had emerged finally successful. But these victories were not the most important events of his life. They were the external reflections of inward victories which he had won earlier, mostly in his youth, against the darker forces of his own nature. One such victory, the first and the easiest, was the conquest of his desire for food and drink - a victory which, he noted sadly, not all men achieved, for some continued all through life as slaves to their appetites; and there were few who could not be deflected from the course of wisdom when the proffered alternatives were good food and drink on the one hand or hunger and thirst on the other.

By these internal struggles, struggles for self-control, Odysseus had succeeded in establishing his reason as the effective controller of his emotions and appetites at all times. They were, therefore, the most significant events of his life. It was they which determined his character, and it was through them that he had made himself the man he was. Added together they constituted the substance of his personality. If, therefore, he considered, he were to record the story of these inward struggles, he would describe the development of his own inner self according to a pattern which, when he returned in his next life, he would recognise as distinctively his own.

Odysseus realised that if he were to tell the story of his inward life in plain terms there would be no possibility of his being able to establish his identity later by claiming to have a character that uniquely fitted the story, for other men would be able to make the same claim. There is no difficulty in finding a key to fit a lock the parts of which are all exposed to view. But if he told his story cryptically in the form of a series of fables or parables which he not only would not interpret but would not even reveal to be fables at all, then, when he came again and gave a rational interpretation of the whole series, he would provide impressive evidence of his identity. He would be like a man who opens a concealed door by fitting a key into a lock that no one knew was there because it had been disguised as a piece of ornamental ironwork. And just as the probability of a given key exactly fitting a certain lock by coincidence is a function of the number of separate levers in the lock, so the degree of certainty that Odysseus reckoned he would be able to claim for his new proof of identity would be a mathematical function of the number of separate symbols in his story to which he would be able to attach specific meanings. If these symbols were sufficiently numerous, the proof, he thought, would be well-nigh irrefutable.

But there were two difficulties. The first was that if he concealed the lock too cunningly he might deceive even himself. How could he be certain that when he returned he would recognise the story as an allegory of his former life and not take it, as he intended the rest of the world to take it, as a pleasant but meaningless fairy tale? This problem he solved by incorporating in a crucial part of the story a mathematical device that was designed to arrest his attention and serve as a clue to the whole riddle - a kind of keyhole of a special shape calculated to reveal specifically to himself the existence of the lock behind it.

The second problem was one that he could not solve by himself: how to ensure that the story he was about to tell survived until he returned? That was outside his control. All he could do was to take the best steps he could to see that it endured, and trust that Athene would do the rest. After all, he reflected, it was her plan that he was trying to carry out. For it was through proof of "psychogenic evolution", or the evolution of the mind through the experiences and efforts of successive lives, that Odysseus felt that the blue-eyed goddess of wisdom planned to give Intelligence the ultimate victory over Might.

Odysseus described the story of his inner life in the form of a series of twelve episodes or adventures, each of which purported to be the account of a struggle he had had with some external enemy during his voyage home from Troy to Ithaca.

It was a mixture of fact and fiction. Many places he described were real places on the coasts of the Aegean and Mediterranean seas. [2] Some of the events he described as they had actually happened; but most he made up, drawing material from folk tales that he had heard in the course of his travels in Greece and foreign lands. The story as a whole was calculated to make a particular appeal to the imagination of young boys and to inspire in them a desire to emulate the qualities of resourcefulness, perseverance, fidelity and courage, which he portrayed as characteristic of his hero. In this way he hoped to achieve a double purpose: to make his story endure through the dark night which was fast falling on European civilization, and to hasten the subsequent renascence of a new civilization based on respect for reason, courage, and self-control.

This, then, is the story that Odysseus told.

Notes on Chapter 10 - Eastern Quest

1. In the Epic of Gilgamesh this is how the poet, through the mouth of Utnapishtim (Noah), describes the coming of the Flood:

> "In those days the world teemed, the people multiplied, the world bellowed like a wild bull, and the great god was aroused by the clamour. Enlil heard the clamour and he said to the gods in council, 'The uproar of mankind is intolerable and sleep is no longer possible by reason of the babel.' So the gods in their hearts were moved to let loose the deluge; but my lord Ea warned me in a dream. He whispered their words to my house of reeds, 'Reed-house, reed-house! Wall, O wall, hearken reed-house, wall reflect; O man of Shurrupak, son of Ubara-Tutu; tear down your house and build a boat, abandon possessions and look for life, despise worldly goods and save your soul alive. Tear down your house, I say, and build a boat.'"

(*The Epic of Gilgamesh*. Translated by N.K. Sandars, Penguin 1960)

This is the earliest known expression of the eminently rational 'dualist' philosophy that attributes all phenomena to a continuing conflict between the destructive tendencies of Matter (Enlil) and the creative efforts of Mind (Ea). What is of special interest to us here is that Ea addresses his message to Noah to or through a wall. The German scholar Arno Poebel, who translated the cuneiform texts that were found at Ur by archaeologists from the University of Pennsylvania at the end of the last century, was puzzled by the references to this wall that he found in many poems about the Deluge. "Did there perhaps exist a tale," he asked, "according to which the wall in some mysterious way passed the secret of the gods on to Utnapishtim?" (A. Poebel: *Historical Texts*. The University Museum of Pennsylvania, Publications of the Babylonian Section, Vol. IV, No. 1, 1914, p. 52 footnote).

2. Ernle Bradford in his book Ulysses Found (Hodder & Stoughton 1963, Sphere Books 1967) traced the wanderings of Ulysses as described in the Odyssey in the central and eastern Mediterranean, and claimed to have

identified, after personal visits in small sailing boats, all the places that Ulysses visited, with the sole exception of the Kingdom of Hades. For example, he identified the land of the Lotus-eaters as the island of Djerba off the coast of Tunisia, the land of the Cyclopes as the west coast of Sicily, and Calypso's island as Malta. Not only the geography of the places themselves but the distances and compass bearings of the journeys between them tallied with remarkable exactness with such particulars as were deducible from the Homeric narrative.

Chapter 11
THE ODYSSEY

I. "When I left Troy with my squadron of twelve ships I came first to the land of the Kikons, a hostile people who lived in a rich country. They attacked us, but we defeated them and plundered their city, seizing great quantities of wine and slaughtering many cattle and sheep. After the fray I urged my men to embark again at once, but they were foolishly intent on enjoying their plunder on the shore. They ate and drank all night. In the morning a fresh force of Kikons descended on us and engaged us in battle. This time we were defeated. With difficulty the majority of us made our escape, but not before we had left six men from each ship dead on the shore.

II. "After we departed from the land of the Kikons we sailed south to Cape Malea, but as we were rounding the Cape we were caught by a strong northerly gale which blew us far off our course. After nine days we reached land and put in to shore. It was the land of the Lotus-eaters, a people who do no work but live on the honey-sweet fruit of the lotus plant which causes them to forget all their ills. The first party of men I sent ashore to reconnoitre were persuaded to taste the fruit of this plant, and they at once forgot all about their ship and lost all desire to continue their voyage home. I found them lazing with the Lotus-eaters and had to use force to drag them back on board the ship, so gladly would they have stayed for the rest of their lives, drugging themselves with the fruit of that delicious plant.

III. "At the next place we came to we had a far more terrible experience, although the adventure started pleasantly enough.

We awoke one morning to find ourselves in a natural harbour. It had been a foggy night and we had drifted there without knowing it. The land was an uninhabited island, a fertile pleasant land, well wooded and watered, with many sheep and goats feeding on the hillsides and in the meadows. We went ashore and enjoyed ourselves, killing many animals for meat and stocking ourselves with a rich supply of fruit and vegetables.

"The mainland was a short distance from the island. I knew it was inhabited because I could see smoke from fires and hear the voices of men shouting to their herds. But it seemed to me the inhabitants must be a backward race because there were no houses to be seen, only caves in the hillside; and they had no boats, for otherwise they would have been able to reach the island.

"So I decided to go ashore and show these cavemen how I was superior to them in every way. I did not know then that they were not men at all but the terrible Cyclopses, sons of Poseidon, a race of ferocious one-eyed giants who live lawlessly, each one by himself, caring nothing for their neighbours or even for the gods themselves.

"Leaving the rest of the squadron in the harbour, I took my ship across from the island and disembarked with a picked band of twelve men, taking with us a skin full of good wine. There was no one about when we landed. We climbed a hill and found a cave, which we entered. Inside a fire was burning and there was a goodly store of cheese and pails full of milk. We helped ourselves to the milk and cheese and were on the point of making off when the Cyclops arrived, driving his sheep in front of him. Leaving the rams outside, he drove the ewes into the cave and then closed the entrance with a huge boulder. As he sat down to milk the animals, he noticed that some of his cheese had gone, and then he looked round and saw us at the other end of the cave.

"'Who are you?' he roared, 'and what are you doing in my cave? This is the home of Polyphemus. No man can enter here and take my food and live.'

"I told him we were sailors homeward bound from Troy who had been shipwrecked off his coast. I implored him to have pity on us in our plight, and asked in the name of Zeus, protector of travellers, if he would give us a little cheese and let us go on our way.

"At that he laughed a savage laugh. He put out his huge hand, seized two of my men and ate them, bones and all, and washed his meal down with draughts of milk. Then he laid down and went to sleep.

"Drawing my sword I would have killed him then and there, but I checked myself because then we would have been buried alive inside the cave, for all of us together could not have shifted the great boulder from the entrance.

"So we lay in fear all that night. The next day the Cyclops arose and drove his sheep out of the cave, shutting the door behind him to keep us imprisoned. While he was gone I devised a stratagem. Standing against the wall was a thick stake of green olive wood which he had cut for a staff. This I took, cut off a length with my sword, then sharpened it to a point and hardened the point in the fire. Then I hid it away and waited for Polyphemus to return.

"He came back in the evening as before, driving the ewes into the cave and again shutting the door behind him. Again he took two of my men and ate them. But this time I came forward boldly, and offered him a bowl of wine to wash down his grisly meal. He took it and drank it in one gulp.

"'Pray, give me some more,' he asked, smacking his lips, 'and tell me your name, that I may give you a present, for your wine is good.'

"'My name,' I said, 'is Nobody. That is what I am called by my mother and father and by my friends.'

"'Very well, Nobody,' he said. 'Now I shall tell you what present I am going to give you. Your present is to be eaten last, after all your companions.'

"At this he laughed again his savage laugh, and then lay down and fell on his back into a drunken sleep.

"Now was my chance. With the help of four of my companions I took the stake and heated the point in the fire until it was red hot. Then we held it over the Cyclops' head and plunged it deep into his eye.

"With a yell he leapt up and plucked the burning ember from his eyeball. Maddened with pain he lashed this way and that about the cave, but he was blind and we easily eluded him. Then he called to his neighbours to come and help him. They called back to him:

"'What ails you Polyphemus? Who is hurting you that you cry out aloud and disturb our sleep?'

"'Nobody is hurting me and doing me to death,' he replied.

"'If nobody is hurting you, you must be mad to cry like that,' they said. 'Be quiet, then, and let us go back to sleep.'

"So they went away; and I chuckled to myself at the success of my trick.

"When dawn came Polyphemus groped for the entrance to the cave, pushed the stone away and sat there while his sheep went out to the pasture. He was determined not to let us escape, and he felt with his hands along the backs of the sheep as they passed him. But I had tied the animals together in threes and under the centre one of each a man was hiding, clinging to the fleece under its belly. I chose for myself the ewe with the thickest fleece of all, a gentle creature who bore me nobly, last of all, past the groping hands of the Cyclops. In this way we escaped from our imprisonment. Once outside we released ourselves and drove the sheep down to the ship, where the rest of my men were waiting for us anxiously.

"As soon as we were all aboard we rowed hard to get away from that baleful shore, but before we were out of earshot I could not resist calling back to Polyphemus and boasting: 'So he was not such a weakling after all, this Nobody whom you thought to devour so easily in your cave. If anyone asks who blinded you, say it was not Nobody, but Odysseus, son of Laertes, King of Ithaca, the man who sacked the citadel of Troy.'

"Hearing my voice the Cyclops seized a huge rock and hurled it at our ship. It narrowly missed us, falling just in front of the prow, and drove the ship back onto the shore with its wash. We pushed off again quickly, this time being careful to keep silence in order not to provide the giant with a second target. But he must have heard the sound of our oars. As we rowed away I heard him utter a mighty curse, calling on his father Poseidon to avenge the wrong that Odysseus had inflicted on him. Alas, as I was to learn later to my cost, Poseidon heard his prayer and answered it. Thenceforward I was relentlessly pursued by the seagod's anger, and would have perished miserably had I not been saved by the mercy of the blue-eyed goddess, Pallas Athene. The Cyclops then picked up another huge boulder and hurled it into the sea. This time it fell just astern of the ship, and the waves it sent up drove us forward on our way to rejoin the rest of our squadron.

IV. "Our next landfall was the floating island of Aeolia, the home of Aeolus whom Zeus has made keeper of the Four Winds. He is a hospitable king who lives with his family in luxury and takes delight in entertaining strangers. For a whole month he entertained me and my companions and many an evening we enjoyed at his sumptuous board recounting to each other the tales of our adventures. When at last we took our leave he conjured up for us a gentle westerly breeze to take us home to Ithaca. The four strong winds he bottled up for our journey, tying them up inside a great leather bag which he stowed away in the hold of my ship with instructions that it must not be untied until we had come safely home to our native shore.

"But his kindness was of no avail. For after we had sailed nine days with the breeze and were within sight of Ithaca, on the tenth day as I lay asleep my men plotted together against me. They were envious of the booty that I was taking home and they coveted the gold and silver which they thought Aeolus had given me as a parting present. With these evil thoughts they untied the leather bag. Out flew the four winds, and at once a tempest arose and tossed our ships far out to sea again.

"Driving us hither and thither for many days, the gales blew us all the way back to the island of Aeolia. But this time Aeolus was far from hospitable. When I explained what had happened and appealed for his help once more he was deaf to my entreaties and sent me packing, calling me a foolish captain of an undisciplined crew.

V.   "The winds now took us to the land of the Laestrygonians, where we found an excellent harbour, closed in on all sides by cliffs, with two headlands facing each other at the north, leaving only a narrow channel in between. The other captains steered their ships straight into the harbour and tied up in the sheltered waters within. But I stayed outside and tied my ship to a rock at the end of one of the headlands. Then I sent a party of three men to reconnoitre and find out what manner of people lived here. They climbed a hill and outside a town they fell in with a girl who was drawing water from a spring called Artakie. She turned out to be the daughter of Antiphates, the King of the Laestrygonians, and she directed them to the palace. There they were taken in to the hall where

Antiphates was sitting with his wife, two huge man-eating giants of terrible aspects. My men were so terrified at the sight of these two that they were struck dumb and dared not even say who they were. Antiphates roared at them, and when they did not answer he seized one of them in his hand with the intention of eating him up. The other two fled.

"Meanwhile other Laestrygonians had discovered the ships in the harbour and began attacking them by throwing huge rocks down from the cliffs. My men were unable to reply. One by one the ships were broken up, and the men struggling in the water were speared by the Laestrygonians like fish with harpoons, to be cooked and eaten. There was nothing I could do to help them. I cut the hawser of my own ship and yelled to the crew to row away as fast as they could. We were thankful to escape, but deeply grieved for the loss of so many good comrades.

VI. "We came next to the island of Aeaea, the home of the beautiful Circe, a formidable goddess skilled in magic, with the body and voice of a woman. She is a sister of the wizard Aeetes, both being children of the Sun by the daughter of Ocean. Aeaea is a densely wooded island, covered by forest trees. When we had beached the ship I climbed a promontory and in the centre of the forest I could see the roof of a house from which smoke was rising. But my men were afraid to move from the beach, remembering the disasters that had befallen us with the Cyclopses and the Laestrygonians. So for two days they stayed by the ship, but I went into the forest and killed a stag and brought it to them to sate their hunger.

"When they had feasted I divided my company into two parties and proposed that we draw lots for which of the two should explore and find out to whom the island belonged. One party I put under Eurylochus, my second-in-command, and the other I commanded myself. The lot fell to Eurylochus, and he set off accordingly, with many misgivings, into the forest. In due course they came to the house where Circe lived. Outside it were many wild animals, lions and wolves and bears, which came up to the men and fawned on them, wagging their tails and behaving like human beings - which, indeed, they were, having been turned into beasts by Circe's magic spells. Inside the house they could see the beautiful goddess weaving at her loom and hear her singing to herself as she wove.

"Presently Circe came out and invited them into the house. They all followed her in, except Eurylochus who stayed outside, fearing a plot. She bade them sit down and gave them a meal of cheese, barleymeal, honey, and wine, but into it she put a powerful drug. When they had emptied their bowls she struck them with a wand and they were all turned into pigs. She then drove them out and penned them in a pigsty where she fed them on acorns and berries.

"After waiting a long time and seeing no men come out, Eurylochus came back and reported to me that they had disappeared. He thought they had been bewitched. He and the others with me then implored me to set sail at once and leave the island, but I insisted on going back alone to find out what had happened. As I was going through the wood I encountered a young man who turned out to be the god Hermes in disguise. He told me all about Circe and her magic, and instructed me how to deal with her. He gave me a drug called moly, a plant with a white flower and black roots which is difficult to dig up. This would make me proof against Circe's drugs, and when she struck me with her wand I was to draw my sword and threaten to take her life. She would then invite me to share her bed, and I must not refuse, but first make her swear on oath to restore my men to their human shape and let them go.

"When Hermes had gone I went on to Circe's enchanted house, and did everything as he had told me. When the goddess found I was proof against her charms she knew who I was and entreated me to sleep with her. This I did after she had sworn as I instructed her. She carried out her oath faithfully and the pigs were taken out of the pigsty and restored to their human form, seeming younger and more comely than before. I then sent for Eurylochus and the rest of my company, and we were all happily reunited with our lost comrades in Circe's hall. That we might rejoice the more in comfort, Circe's handmaids bathed and anointed us and gave us fresh bright clothing. Then she prepared for us a sumptuous feast at the end of which she addressed me by my royal titles and invited me to stay with my company in her house for good.

"We stayed for a whole year. Then my men became restless with desire to reach their native land, and I besought Circe to send us on our way. This she did after giving me prophetic advice how to escape from the many dangers that Poseidon, in answer to the Cyclops' curse, had prepared to lure me to my death. First of all she instructed me that I must visit the house of Hades and Persephone, and speak there with the souls of the dead. On that grim errand I now embarked, and the goddess sent a favouring breeze to speed me on my way.

"But we did not leave the enchanted island without a casualty. One of my men, Elpenor, an earnest but not very practical young man, had gone up onto the roof of the house in the early morning to pray the gods for a safe voyage. The rest of us meanwhile were busy on the ship testing the sheets and halyards stowing the provisions and making sure that everything was in order. When we called to him to come he walked to the edge of the roof, his eyes still gazing heavenwards, missed the ladder and fell and broke his neck.

VII. "I found the kingdom of Hades as Circe had said, on the far side of the stream of Ocean which surrounds the world. There I sacrificed to the dead, and I spoke with the ghosts of my departed comrades and other heroes of ancient times. I saw also my dear mother Anticleia and tried to embrace her, but she slipped through my arms like a shadow. So soon as life has left the body, she told me, the spirit flies forth like a dream and hovers near; and she bade me return with all haste into the sunlight and tell what she had said to my dear wife.

"Before I left I caught sight of Minos, son of Zeus, with his golden sceptre, delivering judgements on the dead. And afar off I saw three of the unhappy mortals he had sentenced to eternal punishments. There was Tityos the giant, whose vast body lay stretched out on the ground while vultures pecked eternally at his entrails. Near him Tantalus, tormented by hunger and thirst, was standing in a pool of water up to his neck, with trees laden with delicious fruit over his head; and every time he made an effort to drink the water or eat the fruit it was wafted away out of his reach. Lastly my own ancestor Sisyphus was pushing with all his might on a huge rock which he was trying to roll to the top of a hill; and every time he almost reached the top the weight drove him back, the rock went tumbling down to the bottom, and the unhappy man had to start pushing all over again.

"After these gruesome sights I lost no time in assembling my men together and launching our ship back into the stream of ocean, where a fair wind sped us on our way."

Odysseus' return from the Kingdom of Hades is a suitable place at which to pause and reflect on how these first seven adventures can be interpreted as allegories of battles that his rational mind fought against the carnal forces of his animal nature.

I describe them as I suggest Odysseus might have described them himself in his own words.

I. "My first encounter with the Kikons was the struggle I had as a boy to master greed and intemperance. The plundering of the city and the feasting on the plunder represents how I used to get drunk and gorge myself with food. My defeat by the Kikons who returned the next morning and killed some of my men is the after effect of insobriety - sickness and damage to the liver. Hard experience taught me a lesson and I learned to control my appetite.

II. "The second adventure with the Lotus-eaters is the struggle against laziness. I was naturally a lazy boy and I hated having to stir myself, but I soon realised that nothing worth while could be achieved without effort and I learned how to discipline myself to work.

III. "My third adventure, with the Cyclops, was a gigantic struggle. It was the struggle against pride or conceit, and its companion, anger. The story begins with my awakening after a foggy night in the lee of an uninhabited island. This signifies my birth and dawning consciousness as a small child, when I lived in a mental world of which I was the only inhabitant. No other person figured in my thoughts except as an object to be governed by my will, like the goats I hunted on the island. As I grew I began to realise that other people had wills and feelings of their own. I crossed over to the mainland and began to explore this new world in which I was one of many. But I still thought I was the most important, the only one that mattered. I thought I was somebody. I wanted everything to be the way I wanted it to be and I devoted my energies to trying to make it so. After all, I was the son of a king. I reckoned myself superior to the common crowd and supposed I could behave as I liked with them. This is where I walked arrogantly into the Cyclops' cave and helped myself to his cheese without thinking of asking permission.

"Once when I was a boy I tried to push a bigger boy out of my way, and when he would not yield I hit him. He picked me up bodily and threw me into a pond. I lost my temper and went for him, but he threw me in again. I was hurt. That was when Polyphemus twice seized two of my men and ate them. The incident taught me to control my temper and not let conceit get the better of my reason. The Cyclops represents both pride and anger, and he is one-eyed because pride is blind to all but its own interests. The conceited man can see only one point of view: his own. He wants things to go the way he wants them to go. Like the Cyclops, he does not accommodate his will to others. His mind is lawless and uncivilized, having no regard for anyone but himself. That was my condition until I realised that there were other points of view besides my own and that theirs could be right, mine wrong. It was then that I found I was imprisoned in the Cyclops' cave, which is the prison of Self. In order to escape from it I had first to conquer anger and pride by subjecting them to the control of reason. This is represented by the blinding of the Cyclops by plunging the pointed stake (intelligence) into his eye. Then I had to abase myself in my own eyes. I thought of myself as a Nobody, a person of no account. I learned to see my own faults, not to resent criticism but to profit by it, and to make amends for injuries which I had inflicted. My men and I escaped out of the cave under the bellies of the sheep, making ourselves lower even than the animals.

"In this way I found freedom. Outside the cave of Self I

was no longer the slave of egotistical ambitions but free to think and act as an integrated member of my society. I could see clearly with two eyes, with one of which I saw my own point of view and with the other that of other people. Looking at it with these two eyes the world came into a true perspective. I could see all problems clearly, objectively, and in focus. I had discovered the only route into the courts of wisdom: through the gate of humility. Even after I was free I was sometimes tempted by pride and would boast of my achievements. But I controlled my desire to boast when I found that whenever I did so some act of enmity would be committed against me which set me back, as the first rock which the Cyclops hurled drove my ship back onto the shore; but when I was humble, and held my tongue, the acts of my enemies only served to drive me forward on my course, like the second rock which fell astern of my ship and helped it on its way.

"When the Cyclops cursed me he invoked his father Poseidon, the sea-god with the trident, who represents the forces of the material world and the flesh. He persecuted me relentlessly for the rest of my journey and he nearly defeated me at the end. But I was saved by Pallas Athene, goddess of wisdom, the personification of intelligence. She worked both within me, helping me to devise plans and stratagems to defeat Poseidon's wrath, and without, ordering events beyond my control so as to forward the efforts I made to carry out the will of her father Zeus.

IV. "My fourth struggle was against the winds of Aeolus. The wind-bag is the desire to talk: to seek advice, to disclose information, and to share secrets. It is a desire by which women are more commonly tempted than men, but men have their problems too. I learned by hard experience to keep my wind bag tightly closed, that is to say, to keep my own counsel, uttering only those words which were calculated to speed me on my course. But I observed that many cannot resist the temptation to talk, and that by talking too much they inhibit action. The winds fly out of the bag and blow them about in all directions - everyone gives them contrary advice - and instead of reaching their destination they end up where they started from.

V.   "The fifth struggle was against the opposite peril: the fear of speaking up against men who are stronger than oneself. This is a more pernicious evil. Failure to face and overcome this fear is the reason why the majority of men today are slaves. It was here, therefore, cooped up in the harbour of the Laestrygonians, made dumb by their fear of speaking up against the cruelty of King Antiphates ('he who hates speakers'), that I lost all the rest of my squadron. By fearing to speak up against tyranny men imprison their souls; they chain themselves to the tyrant's will. But I, all my life, kept my soul free. I would not be dominated by another's will. As a boy when my father shouted orders at me I did not obey unless I chose to. Sometimes when I disobeyed he thrashed me, but if I thought he was being unjust I said so. I would not be tyrannised. This I represented in the story by my decision to keep my ship outside the harbour of the Laestrygonians when the rest took theirs inside and were massacred. 'Artakie', the name of the spring which supplied water to the palace of Antiphates means 'dependence'.

VI.   "The sixth encounter was of a very different kind: the adventure on Circe's island. This was my struggle against the fear of the gods. The goddess Circe symbolises religion. At first she is a sorceress, using magic to bewitch men's minds until they are no longer men with freedom to think rationally for themselves, but resemble pigs who swallow indiscriminately whatever fables are fed to them by their priests.

"With the aid of Hermes, the god of measurement, who represents my scientific approach to life, I made myself proof against Circe's magic. The plant moly is Knowledge. It has black roots which are difficult to dig up, because Knowledge is acquired slowly by toil and effort and its sources are deeply buried in the earth. The white flower signified that my knowledge was general, not specialised reflecting only one colour, but all-extensive covering every subject, reflecting all colours equally. The sword with which I threatened Circe is the sword of logic. Knowledge made me proof against superstitious fears; logic enabled me to attack and kill them.

"When I had disarmed it of its magic, religion assumed for me a new aspect. I saw the goddess no longer as someone to be feared but as someone to be loved. I found the truth about the universal God, who is Love itself. Hitherto my mind had been divided into two parts: one part seeking the truth by the dark intuitive route through religion and the other by the open method of observation and scientific inquiry. The first is symbolised by the party who explored the forest, the other by those who stayed on the beach with the ship. I discovered the truth by first staying with the party on the beach and then going through the forest. Both religion and science were necessary for that discovery. Religion is not enough by itself because it is only concerned with the things of the spirit, and most of life's problems are concerned with the material universe.

Science is not enough because it is limited to the observation of phenomena which take place in the three dimensions of space; it cannot satisfy the desire for communion with the divine, nor can it answer the crucial question: Is there life after death?

"When the two parts of my mind came together in harmony I was conscious of great happiness. This is represented by the joyful re-union of the two parties. The men who had been turned into pigs became younger and more comely than before, because those who have followed the path of religion and acted according to its behests will emerge in the end with their souls in better shape than those whose thoughts have been limited to material things. Religion is the guide-rail which the bulk of mankind has to follow to climb up out of darkness into the light. It has been fixed there by the pioneers, the men of intelligence whose eyes can penetrate far ahead into the gloom by which the rest are baffled. They invented gods in order that, by believing in them, men might live in peace amongst themselves and in the fullness of time achieve their own salvation.

"But belief is not enough. Hard work is also necessary. There are some religious people who, when they are confronted by a practical problem, do not cudgel their brains to find a solution but pray to the gods and hope that one will appear. Such people are symbolised by Elpenor ('hopeful') who, when the rest of us were working, went up onto the roof in the early morning to have a quiet time by himself and pray, hoping that the gods would show him the solution to his problems. But when he came down, instead of making sure he had got his feet on the ladder, he continued gazing up to heaven, missed his footing and tumbled over the edge.

VII. "It was Circe, that is to say, religion in the person of my mother, a religious woman, who warned me of my next difficulties, of which the first, my seventh adventure, was the visit to the house of Hades. This represents the struggle to overcome the fear of death - a grim struggle which all have to face, and which would be made lighter by the knowledge that death will be followed by another life. But those who have committed crimes against the gods have reason to fear eternal punishment such as was meted out to Tantalus, Sisyphus and Tityos. The story symbolises how I overcame the fear of death by looking it in the face that night I was out alone with Diomede. I had steeled myself to be prepared to die when I was miraculously saved.

"Minos ('the measurer') represents justice, which is an intrinsic and eternal quality of the natural universe. The punishments meted out to the three wrongdoers were the automatic consequences of their sins. Tityos the giant was given pain as punishment for his cruelty; Tantalus, king of Lydia, hunger and thirst for his greed and insobriety; and Sisyphus, the thief and swindler, was condemned to perpetual hard labour as punishment for cheating others of the fruits of what they, not he, had sown.

We resume now our summary of the Odyssey, giving this time concurrent interpretations of the remaining five episodes of Odysseus' wanderings, of his arrival at the court of Alcinous, King of Phaeacia, and of his ultimate return to Ithaca and the slaying of the suitors.

VIII. "From Hades we returned to Aeaea where I and my crew were hospitably received by Circe, who warned me of the dangers that we yet had to face and counselled me how to overcome them.

"Our next encounter was with the Sirens, beautiful maidens who day and night sing bewitching songs with which they lure men who pass by. They sit in a meadow among the bones of men who stopped to listen and could not drag themselves away. On Circe's advice I plugged the ears of my men with wax and ordered them to row past with all speed. But I myself desired to hear the song of the Sirens, so I had myself bound to the ship's mast in such a way that I could not release myself from the bonds. In this way we sailed past the Sirens in safety.

"The story of the Sirens tells how I conquered the fell demons of self-abuse by whom unwary youths are lured to untimely death. The Sirens' songs are erotic visions and fantasies which from adolescence onwards, well up into a man's consciousness from the deep recesses of his inmost being. They are in fact, a manifestation of the very quintessence of life, delightful in themselves, but dangerous because of the passionate desire which they arouse. Those who yield to that desire and fail to bring it under control are sapped of their strength and become mental and moral weaklings. They are the men whose bones litter the ground which the Sirens tread. For most adolescents, control is obtained by their parents and teachers denying them access to erotic scenes and causing them to expend their energies in hard work and physical exercise. These are the rowers whom I made to row hard past the island with their ears stopped with wax. But in my case this method failed because the desire was too strong and my imagination too vivid.

"After many failures I succeeded in overcoming the Sirens' lure by means of a stratagem. I observed that the time of greatest danger is the twilight time between waking and sleeping, when the rational mind is off duty. That is the time when sexual desire, like a frisky colt released from confinement, breaks loose. If not disciplined it takes control of a man's unguarded body, using his hands to satisfy its tempting but devitalising end. To foil it, therefore, I constructed a kind of harness by means of which my hands were tied loosely to a collar round my neck in such a way that they could not disobey my orders without my regaining full consciousness. The stratagem was successful. Tied to the mast, I did not need to stop up my ears against the Sirens' songs. I could listen, and yet sail past their island unharmed.

IX and X. "Our way now took us through a narrow passage between two cliffs that rose sheer out of the swirling sea. Two fearsome perils awaited us here, called Scylla and Charybdis. First, in a cave high up in the face of the higher of the two rocks lived Scylla, a terrible monster with six heads and six long necks with which she snatched her prey from whatever living things came within her reach. There was no turning back because the only alternative route lay past the Wandering Rocks, and any ship that goes that way is certain to be wrecked either by the boiling sea or by the flames that belch forth from the Rocks.

"Circe had warned me of these dangers, but I did not pass on to my men the warning about Scylla lest they stopped rowing and hid themselves in the hold. As we approached I put on my armour and ordered the men to row past with all possible speed. But the monster had seen us. She reached down with her six heads and snatched six of my best men in her teeth and carried them up, struggling and screaming in agony, to devour them in her cave. In all my wanderings I never beheld a more terrible sight.

"So the rest of us escaped from Scylla, and at the same time we passed safely by Charybdis, a whirlpool that spells death to sailors who pass under the low cliff on the other side. Three times a day Charybdis sucks the dark waters down to the bottom of the sea and spews them up like a cauldron on a blazing fire.

"Scylla and Charybdis represent the two great forces of potential evil to which all life is subject: fear and desire.

Charybdis represents ambition, by which most ordinary people, represented by the rowers, are not unduly troubled. They are more worried by Scylla, the fear of pain, which all people have to face sooner or later in greater or less degree, and from which there is no infallible means of escape. Scylla has six heads corresponding to the six main parts of the body: the head, the trunk, and the four limbs. When the monster seized one of my men with each of her six heads that signified that in the course of my life I had endured severe pain in each of these parts.

"When pain has to be endured it is best not to let one's mind dwell on it in advance, but to face it when it comes, for fear makes it worse. If I had not concealed from my men the full horror of their coming ordeal they might have panicked, and then the whole ship would have been lost.

XI. "Next we came to a place that promised to afford us a welcome respite from our toils and misfortunes, but which proved in the end to be the deadliest peril of any we had to face. This was a sunny island of rich pastures where the sun god Hyperion kept his sheep and cattle. Circe had warned me that on no account must we touch those animals, or the sun god, who sees everything, would visit us with some terrible calamity.

"When we reached the island we had enough provisions on board to last us for a while, and I would have sailed past, but Eurylochus prevailed on me to anchor in a sheltered cove where we could enjoy a meal on the beach and a good night's rest. When we woke next day a violent storm was raging so that we could not put to sea. For a whole month a strong south wind kept us storm-bound. Our food ran out and the men were sick with hunger. I went away for a while by myself to pray, and during my absence the men rounded up and killed some of the cattle. I found them feasting on roast meat after they had sacrificed to the gods. I rebuked them severely, but I could not undo the wrong that they had done.

"When at last the wind abated we put to sea. Then when we were well out of sight of land, a sudden squall hit us. The forestays snapped, the mast fell, and the ship was struck by lightning and wrecked. The whole company perished. I alone survived, clinging to some broken timbers.

"Wind and sea then swept me back past the island and into the strait between Scylla and Charybdis. This time I was on the other side, heading for the whirlpool. Just as my raft was about to be sucked down into the vortex a big wave lifted me up and I managed to catch hold of a branch of a fig-tree that was growing on the cliff over-hanging the pool. I clung there till the timbers were thrown up again, when I dropped back onto them and by rowing with my hands succeeded in steering myself clear.

"The episode of the stealing of the kine of Helios (Hyperion) symbolises the struggle against the fear of penury that I faced when I decided to travel on alone to the Euphrates instead of returning home. It was the fear of hunger; the fear of finding myself without work, without friends, without money or means of subsistence, and of starving to death. Next to the fear of speaking up against their superiors, this fear of penury enslaves the minds and kills the souls of more men than any other force - a fact which is represented in the fable by the shipwreck from which I was the only survivor. For I had faced that fear and overcome it. Most men excuse themselves for the wrongs they do themselves or condone in others by pleading that to have acted otherwise would have cost them their job or lost them money that they could not afford. 'One must live', they say. But they are wrong. They do not have to live. In point of fact, it is better in the long run for a man to die in penury with a clear conscience than to save his life by an act of shame or cowardice.

"Charybdis, which is ambition or desire for wealth and power, is a force to which few men of the rank and file succumb but which is a deadly peril to their captains. The world of politics and high finance is a whirlpool which draws men into it by tempting their desires. It sucks them down into its muddy depths and spews them out again as mangled corpses. The wreckage that swirls round and round in Charybdis is the wreckage of men's souls. The bottom of the vortex where the pull is strongest, is what the world calls the top of the ladder up which men climb to power and wealth. The world's values are upside down. It regards as desirable that which should be shunned, for desire is itself an enemy. The more successful a man is in pursuing his ambition to reach the top of the ladder, the more likely it is that his soul has been wrecked in the process of climbing there. As for myself, I was lucky. Being born to be a king I had no need to climb to power. Wealth indeed tempted me and I would fain have made myself rich, as I could have done with ease if I had neglected my duty in order to follow the path of ambition. I knew that to do so was to sell my soul to Poseidon. So I resisted the temptation and was content to live on the modest income I derived from my land in rocky Ithaca. This is the fig-tree growing on the rock above Charybdis on which I swung myself clear and escaped being sucked down into that deadly vortex. [1]

"Ambition or desire is a force that pulls forward in the time dimension, fear backward. Scylla and Charybdis are opposite perils. The one, high up on her rock, repels; the other, sucking downward, attracts. Fear is the greater enemy of those who serve, ambition of those who rule. Both claim many victims daily. The way of life lies half-way between the two. The man who would follow it must neither be a slave to others nor seek to dominate them. He must conquer fear and ambition alike and steer his course straight through the narrow channel in between.

XII. "Lastly I came to fair Calypso's island where I stayed for seven years, loved and cared for by that fair nymph, yet pining to be on my way. My decision to free myself from that seductive imprisonment and to set off on the treacherous sea on a home-made raft represents the decision I made after a bitter inward struggle, to turn my back on my wife and family and all the people at home that I loved, in order to go east from Troy in search of the truth about the Flood. Calypso ('she who hides') symbolises my desire to return to Penelope and hide with her, away from the arduous task which I felt it my duty to undertake. I called her island Ogygia, because Ogyges was a king whose name is associated with the Greek flood.

"This was the last great mental struggle I endured, and the most painful. For to sacrifice your own comforts and desires is a far easier thing than to turn your back on those you love when they need your help."

The decision that Odysseus made not to return from Troy at once but to go east on a quest which, in the event, was to keep him away from home for seven more years, was a hard one, but it was justified by its results. The geographical knowledge that he acquired in Babylonia confirmed for him the correctness of his memory of the Flood, and inspired him to invent an ingenious way of proving his theory for the enlightenment of posterity. That invention was the story of the Odyssey, with its twelve allegorical episodes and many more constituent symbols, all capable of rational interpretation once the clue had been spotted that the story was indeed an allegory. The probability that all those symbols just happened by accident to be capable of such interpretation was infinitesimally small. (If any reader thinks otherwise let him try to fit similar interpretations to the episodes of the not dissimilar story of Sinbad the Sailor).

Homer's *Odyssey* tells how the hero eventually left Calypso's island on a raft he had made himself; how Poseidon in a last attempt to destroy him wrecked his raft; and how he succeeded in swimming ashore and arrived bruised and bleeding, naked, hungry and exhausted on the coast of the land called Phaeacia. There he crawled up the beach and went to sleep under a bush.

I suspect that the story of Odysseus' experiences in Phaeacia, as originally told by himself in his manuscript, was related in the form of a dream, but that Homer, when he found the manuscript centuries later and came to translate it into his immortal verse, decided in the interest of poetic style to treat the land of the Phaeacians as just one more of the many magical places that Odysseus visited in his wanderings. Be that as it may, Phaeacia is clearly a dreamland that symbolises Paradise, the ultimate state of the world that Odysseus looked forward to when Might, personified as Poseidon, had at last been definitively conquered by Intelligence (Athena), and the whole world had been united in peace under the rule of Reason. The Phaeacian king is called *Alcinous* which means 'strong intellect'.

The dream begins with Odysseus waking to find Alcinous' daughter Nausicaa playing on the beach with her handmaidens. She is naked,, and so is he - a clear echo of the story of the Garden of Eden that Odysseus had doubtless heard during his sojourn in the east. The pattern of life in this Paradise is described by Alcinous thus: "We are not good at boxing and wrestling, but we are swift runners and very good at sailing; we take constant delight in feasting, music, and dancing; and we love clothes and their changing fashions, hot baths, and the pleasures of the bed." [2]

The dream-like nature of the Phaeacian experience is most clearly apparent at the end, when Alcinous sends Odysseus on his way to Ithaca transported in a ship, fast asleep. The Phaeacian crew deposit him gently in a cave on the shore of his island home. Here there is, as it were, a change of key, for the description of the cave is such as to suggest that when Odysseus regains consciousness he is not awakening from sleep but rather being reborn into the real world after death. The cave is sacred to the Naiads, or water nymphs, and it has two entrances, one on the north side for mortals and the other on the south for immortals. It thus symbolises rebirth in a mother's womb, where the mortal body, entering from without, is joined by an immortal soul entering from within, the two together uniting to produce a living child.

The clue to the allegorical nature of the Odyssey as a whole is to be found in the scene where the suitors are feasting in the great hall of Odysseus' palace, and Penelope, having at long last given up hope of her husband's return, has agreed to marry the suitor who proves himself the strongest. She fetches the great bow of Odysseus, and her son Telemachus sets up a row of twelve axeheads in line and challenges the suitors to string the bow and shoot an arrow straight through the twelve shaft-holes to a target at the end. They all try and fail, their strength being insufficient even to bend the bow to string it. Then Odysseus himself, disguised as a beggar sitting by the door, takes the bow and strings it easily. Then he takes an arrow, "and he laid it on the bridge of the bow, and held the notch and drew the string, and with straight aim shot the shaft and missed not one of the axeheads beginning from the first, and the bronze-weighted shaft passed clean through and out at the last." [3]

The twelve axeheads represent the twelve adventures of the Odyssey, and the arrow that Odysseus alone was able to shoot through them symbolises his penetrating mind, by which he reckoned that he alone would be able to discern their meaning in a future life. In order to trigger his memory in that life he incorporated in the story a deliberate flaw of a mathematical nature, which was this: it is impossible to shoot an arrow through twelve holes in a straight line, because however fast the arrow flies from the bow it takes time to reach the target, and its trajectory is bound to be curved under the influence of gravity. Odysseus reckoned that by this flaw his mind would be alerted to the fact that the story was not intended to be taken either literally or as a romantic fairy-tale, but that it had a hidden meaning - a meaning that he himself had hidden.

Notes on Chapter 11 - The Odyssey

1. A possible oriental source for the story of Charybdis and the fig-tree is indicated in the following extract from Bradford's *Ulysses Found*.

   "It can hardly be coincidence that there is an identical correspondence in Indian legend. The hero Saktideva, on his journey in search of the Golden City, reaches the island of the fisher-king, Satyavrata, who gives him a ship and agrees to act as his guide. As they sail onwards they see something ahead that looks like a dark mountain rising and falling above the waves of the sea. When Saktideva asks what it is, the fisher-king replies: 'It is a fig-tree beneath which there is a whirlpool that drags men down to their death'. In this tale, the fisher-king sacrifices himself so that Saktideva can be saved by grasping the boughs of the fig-tree before his boat is sucked down into the whirlpool."

2. Odyssey 8. 246-9.

3. Ibid. 21 419ff, Trans. Butcher and Lang.

Chapter 12

THE AFTERMATH

The generations that grew up in the wake of the Trojan war were perhaps the most miserable in the whole history of western civilization. They witnessed the collapse of the Mycenaean culture in a welter of hatred and civil strife. There are no records of the actual course of events, but we can imagine what happened.

For decades the peoples of the Aegean had been living on the capital of their soil. They had cut down the forests which attracted and conserved the gentle life-giving rain, and now the pastures were parched with drought, and the light soil on the hillsides, already impoverished by over-cropping, was eroded by wind or washed away by sudden downpours. The land could no longer support the teeming populations of the industrial cities. Nor could merchants any longer import food from abroad, for their capital was used up and their foreign markets were ruined. Unemployment set in on a vast scale and with it came famine and pestilence.

Economic disaster bred social upheaval. The cohesive bonds of religion and family life, already weakened by years of war, snapped under the strain. Respect for laws and for the established authorities of State and Church dwindled to vanishing point. In the wake of atheism and cynicism came envy, hatred, corruption, and crime.

To fan the flames of unrest the Heraclids, a mixed community of egalitarian idealists and political malcontents who had established a socialist state among the Dorian Greeks in Thessaly, now returned as an organised and armed force of revolutionaries to spread their subversive propaganda among

120

the starving unemployed. People who were still able and willing to work they forced to come out on strike at the point of the sword.

Strikes and riots culminated in revolution. The armies of the kings, infected by the communist virus, were unable to stem the tide. The rich estates of the ruling families were seized and pillaged and their owners were hacked to pieces. Kings and their royal families did not escape. In one city after another the revolution swept away all vestige of law and order, and the night sky was lit by the glow of royal palaces in flames.

The spirit of revolt spread throughout the mainland of Greece, Crete, the islands of the Aegean, and the coast of Asia Minor. Only the western isles, which included Ithaca, escaped, and, on the mainland, the two cities of Athens and Tiryns. The fact of their escape has been established by archaeologists, but the reasons for it can only be guessed at. Attica was probably saved from invasion from without because of the poverty of its soil and its geographical location away from the route followed by the invaders from the north whose aim was to seize the richer lands of the Peloponnese; [1] and it may have escaped revolution from within because its wise King Theseus, who had been a keen admirer of his kinsman Heracles, had given his country a democratic constitution which had inspired the Athenian people with such love for their country that they were proof against communist propaganda and stood together in unity against foreign ideologies. Tiryns may have escaped because it was a massively fortified city with cyclopean walls and would thus have been the most likely place to be chosen by the rulers of Argos for a last-ditch stand against an enemy. It can be assumed that kings of the line of Tydeus would have had no scruple in using the most savage means for suppressing any attempt at mutiny by their own forces or assault by armed or unarmed mobs from without.

The destruction of the royal estates only added to the misery of those who wrought it. When all the cattle had been slaughtered there was neither meat nor milk. The rabble wandered about the country like a swarm of locusts, eating all they could find and leaving the country bare behind them. No property was safe from their depredations. Their kings and rulers slain, no vestige of legitimate force remained to protect the innocent.

At this juncture, when all was black despair, a man came forward with a new idea and offered himself as a leader of those who still clung to the principles of ordered society. Seeing that the gods of the established religion were now held in contempt, and realising that without religion there was no possibility of re-establishing order, the new leader's idea was to proclaim a new god, whose prophet he claimed to be, and to announce that this god had promised to lead him and those who would follow him to a new land of plenty beyond the sea. The man was a sailor named Philistos, ('fond of sailing'), and the name of the god he proclaimed was 'Dagon', an ancient Babylonian deity. The people who adopted his faith and followed him are known to history as the Philistines.

The new religion spread because it filled a spiritual need. The Philistines collected their possessions together and left their homes to follow where their leader, guided by his god, led them.

A motley assembly from every part of the Mycenaean world - men, women and children with their animals and all their belongings - collected in Caria in south-west Asia Minor and set off eastwards along the coast. A horde perhaps a hundred thousand strong, they marched or rode with their baggage in carts drawn by oxen, while a multitude of ships accompanied them by sea.

Following the coast, they turned south round the Gulf of Issus through Syria and continued as far as the frontier of the New Kingdom of Egypt. Here a great force under Rameses III went out to meet them. A double battle was fought in which the Egyptians defeated the Philistines by land and sea. A vivid record of the slaughter can be seen today, carved on the walls of the fortified temple of Medinet Habu, near Egyptian Thebes.[2]

This defeat was interpreted by the Philistines as a sign of their god's displeasure, aroused because they had wrongly coveted the rich land of the Nile valley. It was now clear that Dagon intended them to earn their living hardly, and that the land he had promised them was not Egypt but the arid uplands of the territory which to this day is called after them Palestine. The story of their encounters there with the Hebrews, who had but lately trekked northwards out of Egypt inspired by an identical belief in a divine promise that Palestine should be theirs, is told in the historical books of the Old Testament.

Meanwhile in Greece the darkness was complete. Civilization had ended; it was every man for himself. The strong and the clever survived while the weak and the slow-witted perished. There was no organised defence of life or property.

But men and women still struggled after better times. Even in the midnight of despair a spark of hope remains alight in the human heart. The spark which glowed at that darkest hour in Europe and which slowly spread its warmth until it kindled into the bright flame of the Hellenic civilization, was a faith that was built round stories of the heroes of the Mycenaean age, their courage, their cleverness, and their loves, and the evidence which those stories provided of divine interest in human affairs. Chief amongst these inspiring tales were those of the wrath of Achilles and of the wiles and wanderings of Odysseus, repeated by word of mouth from generation to generation as Odysseus himself had told them to his grandchildren.

Some four centuries after the Trojan war, body and soul were given to these tales and new life was breathed into them by the genius of a blind poet. Divinely inspired, Homer searched for and found the precious manuscripts that Odysseus had left, and translated them into the immortal verse that still gives inspiration today.

The purpose that moved Homer to compose the *Iliad* and the *Odyssey* was surely the same as that which inspired another blind poet in a later civilization to compose two great epics telling the story of the struggle between God and Satan. John Milton (1608-1674) stated his purpose in writing *Paradise Lost* and *Paradise Regained* in these words:

> That in the height of this great argument
> I may assert eternal Providence
> And justify the ways of God to men.

Even so might Homer have proclaimed his intention in composing the two great epics which became the spiritual mainspring of the Hellenic civilization, and out of which our own was born. The books of the Iliad and the Odyssey were to the Greeks and Romans what the books of the Old and the New Testaments of the Bible have been to Christendom.

Notes on Chapter 12 - The Aftermath

1. "Attica, of which the soil is poor and thin, enjoyed a long freedom from civil strife, and therefore retained its original inhabitants." *Thucydides* 1. 2.

2. The dating of the events referred to in this chapter, namely the sack of Troy, the Dorian invasions, and the migration of the "Peoples of the Sea", is the subject of controversy among scholars. For our purpose here the exact dates are not important, nor does it matter whether the Dorian invasion took place before or after the migration. Those two events are clearly both symptoms of the same anarchic state of the Hellenic world that followed the Trojan war. 'Philistos' is not a character known to history. I deduced his existence in order to account for the Philistines.

Chapter 13
EPILOGUE

If the mind of the author who has offered in these pages a rational interpretation of the fables in Homer's Odyssey, is indeed a later manifestation of the mind that invented them - if, in other words, what I described in the Introduction as a 'practical experiment' has turned out to have been also a successful experiment - then we might expect to find that the minds of some of the other actors who took part in those dramatic events in the twelfth century BC, are likewise recognisable in new incarnations in the twentieth century AD.

In the first chapter of LIVES RELIVED I listed a number of guidelines designed to assist generally in the search for pairs of characters that can reasonably be identified in successive incarnations. One of these guidelines estimates the normal orbital periods of 'heavy-weight' souls as something between ten and twelve centuries for complete orbits BC, and double that length of time for orbits beginning in the Christian era. On this basis, the three thousand years that have elapsed from the time of the Trojan War to the present day amounts to only two complete orbits for such lives. I regard it as unlikely that the minds of many of the heroes of that war will have changed beyond recognition during that period.

In Appendix I of the same book I reported the unexpected discovery that, when the names of some of the famous characters of antiquity are compared with those of their presumed modern counterparts, the results show that in a significantly higher number of cases than can be accounted for by random chance both the vowel sounds and, more especially, the consonants of the two names of a given pair are markedly similar. The letters and syllables, however, are generally arranged in a different order, and allowance must be made for the interchangeability of related consonants such as D and T, L and R, and M and N.

Thus, the name of the Carthaginian general HAM-IL-CAR and his son HANN-IB-AL are recognisable in those of their nineteenth century Egyptian counterparts MO-HAM-MED ALI and his son IB-RA-HIM Pasha; and the two names of the Roman dictator SULLA FELIX (when the first is pronounced to rhyme with 'fuller') are likewise recognisable in the surname of the American dictator-president F D ROOSE-VELT.

Applying these rules to the heroes of the Trojan War, can we identify a modern warrior whose mind can be compared with that of the swift-footed but proud and uncooperative leader of the Myrmidons, ACHILLES - the hero who sulked in his tent when insulted by Agamemnon, and who refused to take further part in the fighting until a deputation of leading princes came and begged him to save the Greek army from disaster? Can we not recognise him in the long-legged, proud and uncooperative leader of the Free French forces, General Charles DE GAULLE, exponent of the tactics of speed in tank warfare, who, when rejected by the French people in 1946, left Paris and retired to his chateau at Colombey-les-deux-Eglises, confident that the time would come when men would call and beg him to return to save his country from disaster? Not only the characters but the two names are almost identical.

There is no similarly close parallel in modern history to the name of AGAMEMNON, Commander-in-Chief of the multi-national forces that besieged Troy, but that of EISENHOWER, Commander - Chief of the multi-national Allied Forces in Europe in World War II, has the same unusual rhythm. The Greek, as chairman for ten years of a council of kings with discordant personalities, rife with jealousies and mutual distrust, would have acquired a rich experience in diplomacy. This could be seen as having borne fruit in the

American's innate diplomatic skill in the handling of disagreements between rival generals and national governments in both war and peace. But when it came to devising practical plans for military victory, both men showed themselves devoid of ingenuity; and when uncertain how to counter a dangerous threat from an enemy, neither of them could think of a more effective response than to send out spies, or spy planes, to ascertain the enemy's dispositions.

The hostility to the western powers that was displayed by the Arab leader President NASSER of Egypt, his flouting of international law by nationalising the Suez Canal, and his action in proclaiming the union of Egypt and Syria in the United Arab Republic, are the more readily understandable if we interpret them as echoes of the experiences of HECTOR, the doughty leader of the Afro-Asian powers, who negotiated the union of Troy with the Thracian Chersonese and provoked an international crisis by declaring the Dardanelles a national waterway.

Lastly, with whom shall we compare that formidable warrior Diomede, son of Tydeus? Where, in the modern world, might that pitiless and vindictive mind be giving rein to its overweening ambition; and who might be the latter-day victims of its cruelty?

Can it be just a chance coincidence that the name DIOMEDES comprises S, M and two Ds, the same four consonants as of that ruthless tyrant SADDAM Hussein? And can it be no more than a coincidence that Diomede's ambition to annex the kingdom of Sparta gave rise to the world's first successful experiment in collective security, whilst Saddam's ambition to annex the sheikh-dom of Kuwait prompted the launching against him of the first great collective armada ever assembled by United Nations in historic times?

Guideline 6 in LIVES RELIVED states that errors which a person regrets having made in one life he instinctively avoids in later incarnations. If this is right, it would seem that for the rest of his life Diomede bitterly regretted his failure to stand up in defiance of the assembled princes when they prevented him from receiving the prize to which, as the true winner of the games, he was entitled by the normal rules of international law. The injustice and the humiliation of his defeat by a trick so rankled with him that when, in a later life, he was again tricked, as he thought, into believing that the prize he coveted was his for the taking, he instinctively decided he would rather die fighting alone against the world than again suffer the humiliation of surrender.

In the Graeco-Trojan war Diomede was a Greek king fighting on the winning side. Memories of the heroic part that he had played in achieving the Greek victory would have been etched deeply on his subconscious mind in any later life. It could be that those memories were a relevant factor contributing to Saddam's seemingly unshakable conviction that in spite of the overwhelming strength of the forces arrayed against him in the Gulf, his own armies would win in the end. Instinctively, he would expect that, as at Troy, victory would be wrested at the last moment from certain defeat by some kind of divine intervention or miracle.

Perhaps the worst error that any good man ever lived to regret was Agamemnon's decision, taken on the advice of a priest, to sacrifice his daughter Iphigeneia to appease a god. He paid for that error with his life when his wife stabbed him in his bath on his return from Troy. Three thousand years later a kindly Fate gave him a chance to correct that terrible decision. When the departure of the Allied armies for the invasion of France, like the departure of the Greek armies for the assault on Troy, was held up by adverse winds, Eisenhower did not consult a priest. This time he took advice from a scientist, and the departure was delayed for one day only.